A Life Lost . . .
and Found

A Life Lost . . .
and Found

A Journey of Hope and Healing through Tragedy

Wilson   David
Adams   Lanphear

WinePress WP Publishing™

WinePress Publishing (PO Box 428, Enumclaw, WA 98022) functions only as book publisher. As such, the ultimate design, content, editorial accuracy, and views expressed or implied in this work are those of the author.

Scripture references marked NIV are taken from the *Holy Bible, New International Version*˚. NIV˚. Copyright©1973, 1978, 1984 by the International Bible Society. Used by permission of Zondervan. All rights reserved.

Scripture references marked NASB are taken from the *New American Standard Bible*˚, © 1960, 1962, 1963, 1968, 1971, 1972, 1973, 1975, 1977, 1995 by The Lockman Foundation. Used by permission. (www.Lockman.org)

Scripture references marked NKJV are taken from the *New King James Version*. Copyright ©1982 by Thomas Nelson, Inc. Used by permission. All rights reserved.

Unless otherwise noted, all Scripture quotations by David Lanphear, Debbie Lanphear, and Julie Adams are from the **New International Version.**

All Scripture quotations by Wilson Adams are from the **New American Standard Bible.**

All Bible quotations in the Foreword are from the **New King James Version.**

ISBN 13: 978-1-57921-991-8
ISBN 10: 1-57921-991-8
Library of Congress Catalog Card Number: 2009926136

To Julie—
Thanks for holding my hand and heart on a journey of a lifetime.
—**Wilson**

To my dear wife, Debbie—
You brought the sparkle back to my life.

—**David**

This book is written in memory of Adam and Debbie.

". . . till we meet again."

And in memory of Gabriel.

Till we meet for the first time.

Contents

Foreword

Have you been so hurt and felt so low that you could hardly breathe? Have you wondered if you would ever find peace again or if life could offer you just one happier day of existence? Have you ever questioned whether anyone cares? Have you felt so alone; you thought you would never again have joy in a relationship? Have you searched for comfort and found none, even in your prayers?

In this book you will read the stories of four people who experienced your pain. Their lives are not unique . . . but they are special, just as you are special. These are good people. Their pain was not the result of evil in their lives. Like Job of old, they trusted in God. But bad things happened. You know, bad things often happen to good people. Many times, they result from our choices only incidentally.

But when bad things happen, "choices" are forced upon us. How will we handle our adversities? Will we give up? Will we blame God? Will we lose our well-being in depression? What will our character say about us then? What about faith? What about hope? What about love?

A Life Lost . . . and Found is a personal expression of faith in the providence of God. Unlike so many authors who try to explain how people feel—or should feel—during difficult times in life, these authors have all personally experienced every moment of the realities they describe. We can attest to that fact. These people are our dear friends and we have been personally blessed to feel their moments of pain . . . and their times of great joy . . . with them.

God's providence is His overriding vision and His everlasting intervention to supply what we need. Much of the time, He does this through what we might call "general providence." He set up the universe in such a way that He supports human life and well-being through natural law. He makes the sun rise and gives rain to both good and evil people (Matt. 5:45). "He causes the grass to grow for the cattle and vegetation for the service of man" and that provides food for all (Ps. 104:14, 27–28).

But we believe that He also sometimes intervenes into the regular course of things by ordering and arranging the natural forces and the natural environment He created to affect His will when it would not otherwise happen. We call that "special providence." Our assumptions concerning the providence of God are formed, at least in part, upon the Bible's clear call to prayer. We believe in God's providence because we are taught to pray for it. "Be anxious for nothing, but in every-thing by prayer and supplication, with thanksgiving, let your requests be made known to God; and the peace of God, which surpasses all understanding, will guard your hearts and minds through Christ Jesus" (Phil. 4:6–7). His Word encourages us to pray concerning our health (3 John 2), our safety (Matt. 24:20), our nourishment (Matt. 6:11), national peace (1 Tim. 2:1–2), and even our business prosperity (James 4:13–16).

We sometimes need God's presence and His help in times of severe heartache and suffering. Those painful times eventually come to us all. Where would we be without Him? Who else can make it better? To whom can we go when it seems we are so alone? The authors of this book consistently remembered the Lord in their sorrowful times, and they encourage you to do the same.

THE REASON: "There is light at the end of the tunnel." This book is about hope! It says, "You have a future." It does not propose to promise what your future will look like when you emerge from the darkness. But it reminds us that God is in His heaven and He has reserved heaven for you! While it may appear that you are alone and that everyone has left you, God is there! God loves you. And God is going to take care of you. Remember—*He* said, "I will never leave you nor forsake you." Because of that, *you* can boldly say, "The Lord is my Helper; I will not fear" (Heb. 13:6–7).

We think you will shed some tears as you read this book. You may even relate your own story to theirs. But keep reading because the way it turns out will be an encouragement to you. Before you are through, you, too, will smile! And you can believe that if you choose to serve Him, God will bless you beyond all that you can ask or think.

—Colly and Lynda Caldwell
President, Florida College, Tampa, Florida

Acknowledgments

WILSON

Thanking people is a risky venture, but one I must take. I am indebted to all who painfully shared their stories and their hearts. Your struggles and the faith in which you have overcome are nothing short of inspirational. To my dad and stepmother, Bobby, your personal steps of courage through loss were being watched. To Martin and Joanie, brother and sister-in-law, a rock of support. To Bruce McDonald, you were there from the beginning and your wisdom was invaluable. To Phillip and Lori Mullins, you went the extra mile for my kids. To Colly and Lynda Caldwell, who have watched our family saga for years and offered continued support. To Terry and Bev Slack, your friendship means everything. To Brent Lewis, my previous editor, for using your red pen so freely while initially proofreading the manuscript. To Athena Dean, George Dillaway, and the great folks at WinePress, your professionalism and encouragement from the beginning made this a reality. To my children, Sharon, Dale, Crystal, and Luke—my love for you knows no bounds. To my wife, Julie, for encouraging me to write and refusing to let me quit. To our wonderful church family at Cason Lane in Murfreesboro, Tennessee—thank you for loving us as we are. Finally, to my friend, David Lanphear, without whom this book would never have happened and . . . to his *Blue Skies and Rainbows* bride, Debbie.

What began around a kitchen table, followed by long hikes in the great northwest, and writing sessions that pushed us both, this book has finally landed in your hands. It is my prayer that these pages will help every lost life to finally be found.

<hr>

DAVID

I cannot identify and thank everyone who helped make my story and this book possible, but I must mention a few. I first owe a sincere debt of gratitude to those who shared glimpses into the pain and suffering they experienced. May their courage lift the hearts of others. To our church family and countless friends—your love and prayers sustained us. To Alice Gentry Ward, Ed Gentry, Scott Gentry, and Lori White and their families—and to my family, whose hearts broke with mine when our grief was at its worst. To my brothers, Charles and Don, and their wives and children, for doing what I couldn't, especially when days were darkest. To Colly and Lynda Caldwell, who are now integral characters in the story of my life. To the WinePress Publishing family, for your tireless efforts to put our words into print. To my sister-in-law, Beth Fuller, whose wise suggestions made me a better writer. To Hubert and Ann Reeves, who quietly encouraged me to finish this project. To my bonus sons, Michael and Nathanael—you opened your hearts and made me part of your lives. To my sons, Kyle and Colin—I've loved you since the moment you were born. To my co-author and dear friends, Wilson and Julie Adams—you shared my tears and helped me smile, and urged me to start living—and writing. And finally, to my loving wife, Debbie—without your courage to share your story, this book would not be the same; without your encouragement and counsel, I never would have finished. Thank you, sweetheart. May those who hurt find comfort in these pages, and may God be glorified in all things.

Introduction

There was a tinge of winter in the air the day we decided to tackle the hill. We were hiking in Yellowstone National Park, not far from the famous Old Faithful, when David asked if I was up to the climb. The small twin peaks rising above us looked relatively harmless from below and only a moderate climb for a couple of mid-life guys in halfway decent shape. Besides, I have always had a quest for adventure and an ever-present curiosity to discover what's over the next hill. David laid down the gauntlet and I picked it up.

We started climbing while the other guys in our hiking party (with much more sense than we obviously had) watched from below. It's funny how small a hill can appear when you're only *considering* the ascent. Tackling the project is another matter entirely. Like two kids whose eyes are bigger than their stomachs, we took off for the top, determined to make it and too embarrassed to back down.

And we did make it although we took different paths to get there.

Standing on the crest of the rise, I anticipated a moment of deserved rest and exhilaration—perhaps shooting some pictures and taking in the 360-degree view from such a lofty vantage point. After all, co-king of the hill deserves some kind of reward after such an expenditure of effort. It didn't exactly turn out that way.

Out of breath (and perhaps out of my mind), I topped the little rise and came face-to-face with a 2000-pound buffalo bull. He startled me and I startled him. I'm not sure which came first. But it didn't matter. They say that what goes up must come down and I can attest to the validity of that observation. I can also attest to the truth that one can descend with greater rapidity than one can ascend. A disturbed buffalo bull can give you that sense of added urgency. David, on the other hand, was braver than I. He hesitated, and then faced the beast with the only weapon he had, a digital camera. He clicked some pictures before hastily joining me on a descent to a lower and wiser elevation.

Our lives are very much like that, and the story of this book could be summed up by our experiences on the mountain that day. In facing the difficulties of life, there are times when you think you can handle anything, but the reality of the challenge is often far more than you bargained for. Some give up before they ever get started. Others fight through the trauma of human tragedy and claw their way to the top, anticipating a period of deserved peace and smooth sailing, but what they get instead is another mountain much higher than the last. And sometimes, just when you think you're at the top and things couldn't be better, you get the shock of your life.

But that's life. For David. For me. And probably for you, too.

Our stories are unique in one way but common in another. This book is the story of human suffering told from the vantage point of people who have faced incredible loss—different loss but loss all the same. I wish I could tell you that the path up the mountain has been easy for me. It hasn't. And my friend will tell you the same. But you can't quit. You can't quit climbing, or hoping, or believing—believing that the power of God can equip you for whatever challenges you face, or will face in the future.

This book is not for quitters. It is not for people who have pulled the curtains and drawn the shades and given up because life is hard. Yes, life is hard and some days it gets harder. Listen, if my friend can fight through the adversity he has faced and is facing, then so can you. His story inspires me. And maybe my story will help you, too.

Let's climb that mountain. Together.

Chapter 1

Lives Lost

WILSON

I have been writing "my story" for the past eighteen years; I just have never put it on paper. I'm not sure why, unless the process of opening up old wounds was too painful. I have wished many times that "it" would just go away. But "it" hasn't. And "it" won't. And "it" never will.

I am divorced.

Like the alcoholic who finds the courage to stand at his first A.A. meeting and admit what he would rather hide and deny, well, that's me. It's not easy to tell you this, or admit it to others or even to myself. But it's true.

I am divorced.

You may wonder why it's that big of a deal. After all, over half of all marriages end in divorce these days and it is a rather common thing for people to talk in flippant tones about an ex-husband or ex-wife as if they were speaking about a once-loved vehicle they traded in for a newer model. I hate that. My view of marriage is one of permanency and lifetime commitment. One man and one woman *"until death do you part."* That is what I wanted and that is what I intended. But along the way I had to learn a very critical lesson—you can't *make* someone else remain committed, nor can you make him or her do what is right. You can only control yourself.

It's been a difficult struggle. Divorce always is. It has been described as "the gift that keeps on giving," and anyone who has been on the receiving end of a judge's gavel knows exactly what that means. It just never goes away.

I should also tell you something else: I am a minister. There were days when I wished I wasn't. There were days when I felt the extra burden that accompanies the glass house in which most of us who fill pulpits are forced to live. And there were days when, even though I was innocent of any wrongdoing, I wondered if people believed me and if they would have confidence in my work. It was an added burden and certainly not an imaginary one.

I am divorced.

Almost two decades after the fact, it is still hard to admit. There comes with that word a sense of failure, and although God does not hold us accountable for the sins of another, sometimes people aren't as merciful. But I can't do anything about that. And neither can you.

June 12, 1990

I was thirty-two years old with a wife and three children, a mortgage, and a promising future. We lived in a typical big-city suburb and faced the usual joys and trials that accompany couples experiencing twelve years of marriage. There had been some bumps in the road but things seemed okay. Until that night.

I stayed home with the kids so that my wife could have an evening out with some church friends. After playing with our three children—ages nine, eight, and eighteen months, and following baths and bed-time stories, I was getting rather tired myself and a little concerned that the familiar headlights of the station wagon had not pulled into our driveway. I washed up and decided to grab a book and do some reading in bed. I pulled back the covers—and found the note.

Do you know the feeling when your heart stops and you experience a sense of nausea, wishing you could throw up but nothing is there? And do you know the sensation you get when you know, you just know, the news is bad even before you ever pick up the phone or read the letter?

I knew. I knew even before I read the first line.

Five years before my wife had asked for a divorce. That one, I hadn't seen coming. My mother had only recently died at the early age of fifty-four and I was still in the shock of dealing with the trauma of losing a parent much too soon. And now, on the heels of one tragedy, there came another.

Shocked and speechless, I had asked her why. She didn't have a good reason, only that there was someone else, and they had been together recently, and they went way back and . . . It didn't make any sense and I was too numb to be angry. I remember asking her to come with me into our children's bedroom, and standing together we watched the sleeping bodies of a four-year-old little girl named Sharon and a three-year-old little boy by the name of Dale. I asked her how she could do that to them and leave them with a divided home and destroy the innocence of their world. She cried. We walked back into our bedroom and I promised that if she would give me half a chance, I would do my part to work this out. She agreed.

She went and talked with Bruce, a respected and wise older brother in the church. He came to me afterward and said that she had admitted to him that she had not been faithful in our marriage. "You have every right to divorce her for adultery," Bruce said, then added, "but I want you to ask yourself this simple question: 'What would the Lord want me to do?'"

I knew the answer to that question. I had seen the answer to that question in the silent sleeping of our two children. We had to work this out. She asked for forgiveness and I forgave her. As far as I was concerned no one knew or needed to know.

Then it happened again. We had moved that summer to a different house a little farther away from the city. We needed a fresh start and it offered the promise of a newer home in an area where the schools were better and the streets were safer. In the fall of that year, and with little Dale's sister enrolled in kindergarten, I took him with me back to Kentucky to visit with his grandparents while I had a speaking engagement at a nearby church. When we came home from that trip, I knew something was wrong.

I don't know how I knew. I just knew.

My wife admitted that it had happened again. She had allowed him to come to our home and stay during the week I was away. Hidden in a bedroom until our daughter was away in school, he went undetected.

I was sick again. Even to this day it is incomprehensible to me how she could have done that. But she did. What I did next may be incomprehensible to you, but . . . I forgave her. Again.

I know what you're thinking. You're thinking that I was in some kind of denial—and you're probably right. She met with Bruce again and they talked it out. Then we all talked it out. She admitted her weakness and promised—*promised*—that it would never happen again. This was the end, and to prove that her past would stay there, she would write him a letter and terminate the relationship for good.

She wrote the letter and together we mailed it. I chose not to read it. I chose not to read it because I felt that if we were ever going to make it, we had to re-establish trust. Obviously, trust had been shattered by repeated infidelity, but rebuilding trust had to start someplace and this was the place.

Over the next five years I did what I knew to do to be a good husband and dad. Perfect? Hardly. But this was not about perfection. In fact, it never is. It was about a commitment to the permanency of marriage and the fleshing out of what I had been telling others for years. God had forgiven me of many things over my lifetime and, once forgiven, I noticed that He didn't keep bringing it up again. I had to do the same.

Forgiveness is forgetting, so I didn't follow her when she left the house nor eavesdrop on phone calls. I didn't give her the fifth degree when she was a few minutes late or remind her at convenient times of her past. I believed with all my heart that my best course of action was to work to rebuild what had been broken and if she was willing, so was I.

Five years of rebuilding can accomplish a lot. We had our third child, a blue-eyed bundle of joy we named Crystal Dawn. We were growing up together and enjoying our lives. I was busy with my church work, she became involved selling Mary Kay, and the kids were active in school and sports. We took trips, entertained friends, and for the first time in a long time, I sensed that we were finally going to make it.

I was wrong.

The Letter

I opened it slowly. I recognized her handwriting and began to read how she would not be coming home. She admitted being with the same man again, but this time it was different. She needed him, had seen a lawyer, and had been assured that she would get the children. She said that it wasn't about me and indicated that she would come home the next morning to talk.

I remember sitting down on the bedside knowing it was over. After forgiveness and years of trying to make it work and rebuild trust, there was none. My feelings were so complicated and confused I didn't know where to turn. I called my brother in another state. It was late, too late to be calling, but I didn't care, and neither did he. It helped to talk to someone. To this day I don't remember much about that conversation, just that I needed it.

She did come home the next morning. I had already hustled the baby off to stay with some church friends. The older kids had gone to school on the last day before summer break, and thus the two of us sat alone in a house where we had shared the joys and sorrows of married life. I remember that we spoke calmly and I also remember that it was the strangest feeling I have ever had. Twelve years of marriage, yet sitting across the room from each other on that summer day she felt like someone I didn't know. Looking back on it now, there was probably more truth to that than I realized then.

She stated her intention to travel temporarily to another state to be with him. She needed, she said, to get away. I asked if she could wait until the afternoon, as there were some things I needed to do and she agreed.

I found Bruce again, the same friend who had counseled both of us years before, and shared with him the letter. "This is different," I said, "and I'm not sure what to do." My trusted friend and confidant knew what to do and within a few hours we were sitting in an attorney's office drawing up papers for divorce on the grounds of adultery and asking the court for temporary custody of all three children. I had never been in a lawyer's office before nor been as nervous as I was that day. My attorney agreed to file the proper documents the next day.

Traffic was at a standstill on the way home. I kept looking at my watch and thinking about the kids. *They must be coming home about now,* I thought. *I wonder what, if anything, she is telling them.* They say some trips home are longer than others and that was the longest of my life. I pulled into the driveway. Her car was gone.

Opening the door I found our two precious children, Sharon, age nine, and Dale, age eight, sitting alone on the stairs with a faraway look in their eyes that I will never forget as long as I live. "Where's Mom?" I asked. "She left," our brave nine-year-old said. I then found out that Mom, suitcase in hand, had met the children at the door when they came home from their last day of school, and asked them if they knew what "divorce" meant. She informed them that Mommy and Daddy were going to get a divorce and that when she got back from her trip, they would be living with her. She walked out the door, telling them that their daddy would be home soon.

I'm not sure there is a word in any language that can describe the look in their little eyes. I remember dropping my briefcase and grabbing on to each of my kids and vowing before God that I would never leave them and that I would fight for the right to raise them. And I will never forget them hugging me and telling me, "Fight hard, Daddy, fight hard."

I did.

The Aftermath

That was a long time ago. In some ways it seems like yesterday but in other ways it seems like an out-of-body experience from another life. These are the kind of things that happen to others, not me. But isn't that what everyone says about tragedy? Why is it that we think tragedy—death, divorce, or disease—always happens to everyone else? Why are we surprised when it happens to us? And it will happen to us. If it hasn't happened yet, you just haven't lived long enough.

In the years since that June night, life has moved on. Time has helped to heal but even time cannot erase every hurt. I would like to say that after that awful night, the hard part was over. The truth of the matter, however, was that the hard part was only beginning.

If you have ever been through a contested divorce involving children, you know that there is no way to describe the horrors. To stand before a man or woman in a black robe and have them make judgments regarding the future of your children stretches the limits of faith like few things can. To have your person and parenting skills demeaned and degraded by an opposing attorney to the point that you are painted to be someone that even you do not recognize, is very hard to take. And to proceed through the maze of paperwork, court appearances, court-ordered psychological evaluations, postponements, and mounting legal bills is a more daunting mountain than most will ever climb.

Sometimes I look back on that period of time and wonder how I found the strength to survive. There are moments in the midst of a storm when it is not, "Lord, help me get through this day . . ." but "Lord, help me get through this minute," we'll worry about the "day" later. The strength of God, the encouragement of friends, the support of family, and the daily interaction with my children pulled me through. Two verses in the Bible gave me hope:

> Do not be grieved, for the joy of the Lord is your strength.
> —Nehemiah 8:10b

> We know that God causes all things to work together for good to those who love God, to those who are called according to His purpose.
> —Romans 8:28

Through the long and difficult days that followed, those verses provided me with the blessed assurance that my life and the lives of my children were in the hands of One more capable than I. Everything around me seemed to be spinning out of control but that was because my vision was limited. If God could create the heavens and the earth and control the world that He made, certainly He could take care of three little children and their daddy. And He did.

Eventually, on February 19, 1992, I was granted full legal custody of all three children—no small feat given the court's general attitude toward the rights of the mother. Two years later, the court would sign an order allowing me to move with the children to Nashville, Tennessee where I had been invited to begin work with another church. That, too,

was traumatic, but much needed in order to bring stability into a tur-
bulent situation and give us some space that had become too crowded
by the mother's insistence on living so close. At first, she moved five
houses down from ours. When we sold the house and divided up the
assets (that was the easy part), we chose to move to another subdivision
a mile away. She chose to move closer and into the same subdivision.
Feeling rather claustrophobic by her apparent desire to live under our
noses, and sensing the need for a new beginning, we chose to move to
another state and live in a more rural environment.

I have never regretted that decision.

There is one more thing you should know. I remarried. For some time
I was preoccupied with the needs of three small children and ongoing
legal battles in addition to my church work. My plate was full—so full,
in fact, that I was juggling several plates! Adding a romantic relationship to the mix wasn't exactly high on my immediate list.

I don't know when it hit me but it did. I think it was one of those
nights when, after I had read to the children and put them to bed—all
three of them slept in my bed for several months—and while I was up
doing laundry at one o'clock in the morning, it dawned on me that I
needed to begin to take care of me; not to the exclusion of them, but
because of them. If their daddy burned out, in the long run that would
not exactly be in their best interests.

Julie

I always thought of her as a cousin. She wasn't really, but our parents
were so close growing up that we called her dad "Uncle." When we
were kids, her folks would come to the house on Friday nights, and
while the grownups played Rook, Julie, my little brother, and I would
retire to the basement and play church. She always insisted on being
the preacher, I was the song leader, and my kid brother was the sinner.
It worked wonderfully well until one night he got a hard heart and
refused the gospel call. I don't think we played much after that. It's kind
of hard to play church without at least one sinner.

Our lives grew apart and although Julie and I saw each other on
occasion, it was rare. She graduated from college, became a registered
nurse, and had never married. The only snag in this potential courtship,

however, was a big one. She lived two states and three hundred miles away! What began with casual conversations on the phone evolved into brief trips to visit. It's hard to date with much consistency when such a formidable distance separates you, but we did the best we could. Years later we laugh about it. "I had to marry you," I tell her, "I couldn't afford not to."

I would like to tell you that in the years that followed, everything went well. There was a new move, a new wife, and a blended family. We also had a new appreciation for the Brady Bunch—until we realized it is fiction—and not always that comical. But I had found love again and the thrill of discovery that it was returned in a mutual way. Today, the two of us have a special relationship because together we have endured more than we can possibly describe in a hundred books. She means the world to me.

Remember the two scared children I found waiting alone on the stairs all those years ago? They are grown. One of the great blessings of parenting is seeing your relationship blossom with your adult children as you move from the role of parent-authority to parent-friend. And it has. Our oldest daughter, Sharon, met a young man at a private college in Tampa, Florida run by Christians, and in the spring of 2001 they married in our side yard under the giant willow where he had proposed the year before. Her husband, Kyle, went on to become a firefighter and together they bought a home about an hour away. They have also graced our family with a beloved granddaughter: Callie Rose—the absolute delight of our lives (and little Gavin is on the way!) Dale, our oldest son, graduated from Western Kentucky University with a degree in sociology and criminal justice and has gone on to fulfill his lifelong aspirations of law enforcement. He will do well at whatever he does. This past summer Dale married a beautiful young Nashville native named Brittany and they are enjoying the early years of married life.

Crystal, the toddler baby girl, is now twenty, and has a smile and sparkle that lights up the room. She is living and working in College Station, Texas and very much an Aggie.

And finally, God blessed Julie and me with a little extra surprise, a son named Luke, who is thirteen and filled with an abundance of energy and humor. (Why does God give the last child the most energy?)

I mention this because I want to tell you the same thing I have told my friend and co-author of this book: *there is light at the end of the tunnel.* Sometimes you can see it clearly although it appears rather distant. At other times it seems rather dim as troubles mount and hope fades. But it is there. To those of you who are in the process of picking up the pieces, whatever the tragedy—divorce, death, or disease—I say this: the dawn will come and the light will shine again. It will.

Sometimes, however, it is darkest before the dawn.

Just ask David . . .

Chapter 2

The Trauma of Tragedies

DAVID

There is light at the end of the tunnel..."

"Oh, yeah?" you say to yourself. "You've not been in my tunnel."

There *is* light at the end of the tunnel. Believe me. There is.

You're thinking, "It depends on what causes the darkness." Perhaps you have a hard time seeing light in a tunnel so long and in darkness so dark because it's caused by death, the loss of someone very close to you, someone you loved, and perhaps still love, very much.

Death. The word even sounds horrible. It brings menacing visions of shattering grief, unrelenting gloom, and foreboding inevitability. How do we deal with the pain that impacts our lives when death comes to someone we love? What do we do when we are enveloped in a shroud of sorrow so immense we cannot see past it or think of anything else? How do we repair the palpable loss death inflicts on us over and over when we see a date on a calendar, hear a certain song, or smell that familiar scent—when we're reminded that someone we loved will never return and the future we dreamed will never appear? How do we survive such pain and loss and suffering? How can anyone know how to answer those questions?

Well, there is an answer, I believe, for those questions. I don't claim to be an expert on grief, but I am experienced, and perhaps my experience will help you.

What has happened to me is not so unique. Others have gone through the same thing. You will meet some of them in these pages. But you should know—*you must understand at the outset*—others have been where you are or may be headed, others have experienced loss, gut-wrenching, and heartbreaking loss. We have survived and you can, too.

He Who Knows Joy

Debbie and I married in August 1974, just before my senior year of college at Western Kentucky University. I was twenty; she was nineteen; we both were kids. We'd met in January the previous year, and within a couple of months we knew we were meant for each other. She called it love at first sight. I guess she was right.

After I graduated, we moved to northern Kentucky, where I attended law school. During my final year we began to plan for our family like all the other married couples in my class. We naively decided that the best time for the baby to arrive would be a couple of weeks after the July bar exam, so we counted backwards nine months and, according to plan, she became pregnant on the first try. Life was wonderful—not perfect, but pretty close to it.

I cannot recall everything about the delivery room, or much at all, for that matter. I stood at the head of the bed, behind Debbie's right shoulder. I remember an IV drip connected to her arm and a warming tray and light over against the wall. Of course, there were bright lights overhead and lots of medical gadgets and equipment. Her legs were in stirrups, most of her was draped and there was a small round mirror situated just so I could see the birth. The doctor was scrubbed and doing whatever a doctor does at the end of a delivery table. Nurses and attendants (two, three maybe?) were scurrying around to assist him and prepare for our child—we didn't know whether the baby was a boy or a girl. Exchanges between the doctor and nursing staff joined occasional beeps and other "medical" sounds to fill the busy room.

Debbie had been an unbelievable patient during the entire process, breathing, relaxing, and pushing just as instructed by the hospital staff. It was Sunday. This was our first child. Her labor started around 6:30 A.M. and by 8:00, we were at the hospital. We had been through the husband-coached labor classes, and her labor was textbook. Now, on August 13, 1978 at 10:46 A.M., the doctor told her to make her final push: "We are going to have this baby, Debbie. Push, for me. Push." I leaned close to whisper in her ear and assure her it wouldn't be much longer.

She lifted her head and shoulders from the bed in a crunch and grunted with all her might. I could only see the side of her face, but she was working as hard as she could work. There wasn't another ounce of effort left in her. The nurses shouted encouragement.

"The baby's crowned," the doctor reported, and I don't recall what came after that. I knew what "crowned" meant and I focused on that small round mirror. There, in a circle about the size of a baseball, I could see the top of a head come into view. I glanced at Debbie to see if she saw what I saw. I was so excited for both of us, but her eyes were closed tightly as she bore down.

"There it is, sweetheart," I told her. "If you want to see, you *have* to look now." Of course, she was busy. All she could think of was squeezing that baby out of her.

Suddenly, this beautiful baby boy emerged. I was in awe at the miracle of birth. I expected the doctor to swat his bottom to help him start breathing, but instead he pumped air into his nose through a rubber bulb, and our son let out his first cry—a five on the Apgar scale, for those who know what that is. I counted his fingers and toes, and looked over his helpless little body as the medical staff attended him. I stared at his face, his beautiful face. He had a cowlick just like mine. This was *my* son.

I moved around the bed, clasped my wife's hands, and kissed her cheek. We were just inches apart as I gazed into her eyes. "You've done it, sweetheart, you've done it!" Tears welled up in my eyes and ran down her cheeks. It was an extraordinary moment. Those who have witnessed the birth of their children know what I mean.

Outside the delivery room, a nurse took the baby to the warming tray and I asked if I could see him. She said, "Sure" and asked if I was the father. "Father"—the word struck me for the very first time.

"Yes," I said awkwardly.

She smiled. She had done this a lot of times. "Have you decided on a name?" she asked, writing on a clipboard.

"Adam Christopher," I said proudly. I stared at him as he lay there crying in the warming tray. He was so vulnerable and dependent. I placed my finger in his hand, and he wrapped his little thumb and fingers around it. He was *my* son; I was *his* father. Witnessing his birth was the single most exhilarating thing I'd ever done in my life.

He Who Knows Pain

In the years that followed, the good Lord blessed us in many ways—two more wonderful sons, Kyle and Colin, a productive law practice, and many other good things. To be sure, we experienced problems like everyone else, but we worked through them together.

In August 1999 we celebrated our twenty-fifth wedding anniversary and Adam turned twenty-one years old. He was now a junior at Indiana University with plans to enter business school. A couple of weeks after the fall semester started, he called to ask Debbie to schedule a dental appointment for him. He had chipped a tooth and wanted to come home to get it fixed. The appointment was arranged and he came home for the weekend. It was great for him to be home. That Sunday afternoon, September 19, he left to return to Bloomington. We went to church and afterward were invited with several other couples to the home of our dear friends, Johnny and Chesa, to celebrate the arrival of our church's new evangelist.

At around 9:00 P.M., Chesa came and told me I had a telephone call. That was odd. I hurried to the kitchen where the phone lay on the counter.

"Hello?"

"Hey." It was my older brother, Charlie. "Can you come into town?"

I immediately sensed that something was not right, or else he wouldn't have tracked me down or asked me to suddenly leave. "What's wrong?"

I asked quickly. My mother was in relatively good health, but she was seventy-eight years old, and I immediately feared that something might have happened to her. This call was out of the ordinary.

"Well, can you come into town?" he asked again.

"What's wrong?" I said, more persistently this time. I expected to hear him say, "It's Mother."

He halted. This was something he dreaded. "There's been an accident." His words sent shock waves through me.

"Adam?" My voice was urgent. "Is it Adam? Is he okay?" I hung on his answer. Every nerve in my body was on edge. My son was on I-65. An accident at high speed on an interstate highway could not be good. Still, I never expected the response he gave.

"He's deceased." His voice cracked; the words stunned my senses. A profound wave of horror swept through me to the very core of my being. This was *so* unexpected, *so* far from the remotest realm of possibilities. How could my son, my firstborn son, whose light was so bright and whose future was so promising, suddenly be gone?

"No. No," I pleaded in disbelief. "Please tell me it's not true." He didn't reply. I'm sure he was holding his breath, fighting the tears of grief he would share with me. My face contorted, my lips quivered, and I started to moan. I pleaded again. "Please," I begged him. "Please, Charlie, tell me it's not true." I wept the words from my mouth.

"I wish I could, David," my brother said, "but it's true."

Time seemed to go into slow motion. The floor beneath me began to spin. I remember praying, "Oh Father, not Adam. Please let me switch places with him. If there's only a blink of time to do it, please take me, not him." I fell against the wall and then to the floor, unable to stand alone. "Not my Adam," I cried, my chest heaving. "Not my Adam. My son. Oh, my son." I repeated it again and again. I was sprawled on the floor, awash with grief, all life and will to live ripped from my spirit, immune to everything but the crushing pain in my heart.

In a matter of seconds (although it seemed like forever), Debbie rushed into the room. Someone had told her something was wrong. Bewildered, she hurried to me. "Honey," she knelt beside me, "what's wrong?" Her eyes searched me. She saw I was distraught.

How could I tell my wife that our son, our firstborn son, whom we loved more than our own lives, was dead? Through tear-soaked eyes, I looked into her face and wept two words. "It's Adam," I whispered. They were the only words I could squeeze from my lips, but they destroyed her.

The horror now rushed into her face. "Is he okay?" she asked, immediately hoping against hope. She could tell the answer by looking at me.

I shook my head from side to side. My expression said, "He's gone," and she instantly knew what I meant. The terror in her eyes told me so.

"No, not Adam!" she screamed through a sudden burst of tears. She flung her fists at my chest, fighting the horrible news that stole our smiles. I caught her flailing arms and pulled her to me. Together we wailed, rocking in unison in the middle of our friends' kitchen floor. Our hearts were wounded beyond description. Without question, this was the saddest moment of our lives. We had just entered what I call the deepest valley, a great and awful period of despair.

Of course, the news spread quickly through the house. Our friends gathered around us. Johnny or Chesa—someone—spoke briefly with Charlie to arrange for us to meet at the hospital where Adam's body was taken, and they drove us the long, silent trip into town.

Friends began to gather at the hospital. Kyle and Colin met us there, aware that Adam had been in an accident, but unaware that he had died. I had the unpleasant task of telling them so.

We later learned that the left front wheel of Adam's car had slipped off the pavement, probably in a split second of inattention while he reached for a CD from under the front passenger's seat. He overcorrected, lost control of his vehicle, and in a millisecond, veered across the median into the path of an eighteen-wheeler. He died instantly.

This was the darkest year of our lives. We started the tortuous journey through sorrow and loss.

While we didn't want it to, life moved on. Slowly we began to return to our pre-accident routines, though we were mired in grief. The distraction from my practice dramatically reduced our income. Less than a year after the accident, Colin had life-threatening scoliosis surgery. Looking through our eyes, life was a dismal shade of gray. But, as we'll discuss later, we began to recover. Our lives were not the same (and never will be), but we began to find little pockets of happiness in successes here and there. Eventually, a faint hue of color started to return to the palette of our lives.

Kyle went to the University of North Carolina at Chapel Hill and graduated from the UNC Business School. He landed a good job as a consultant with General Electric and traveled extensively across the country. Colin was well-liked by his peers, and despite the physical challenges he faced, was elected student body president during his senior year of high school. In time, my practice and work ethic returned. We were beginning to see the results of healing. As I describe it, we were getting to the point where we could enjoy the holidays again, although it took several years and lots of adjustments.

June 29, 2004

Debbie and I started to travel without the boys as they grew older and more independent. We enjoyed the excitement of new and different places, and treasured the time and companionship we had by ourselves. When 2004 rolled around, we began making plans for a long-awaited thirtieth anniversary trip to Europe. By now, life seemed to be on an upswing. I had just finished a successful year at work, Kyle was working in Raleigh, Colin was graduating high school and Debbie was busy at home, inspired by *Trading Spaces* to redecorate every room in the house.

On June 28, 2004, Colin's wisdom teeth were removed. The next morning Debbie, the always-attentive mother, was waiting on him hand and foot. He sat in our den and drifted in and out of the groggy world of pain medication. She sat with him while they watched a movie together. When it was over, she fixed him a lunch of mashed potatoes and then went outside to work in the landscaping.

Meanwhile, I had a typical day at the office. As usual, I telephoned Debbie briefly mid-morning just to check in. During the lunch hour, I stopped at Home Depot to look for a new weed eater and then went to an Italian fast food restaurant for a quick bite of lunch. After I finished my meal, a friend stopped by my table to visit for a moment. I checked my watch and decided to read a few minutes before I went back to work. It was an ordinary day. Then, my cell phone rang.

"Hello?"

"David, it's Millie," the voice said frantically. "Debbie was found unconscious in your front yard! The ambulance is here now! You need to come home!" Millie was our neighbor two doors down. She spoke so urgently the sentences all ran together. I lurched in my seat. A familiar terror raced through my body.

"Is she okay?" I asked quickly.

"They're working on her now. You need to come home!" Millie rushed.

"I'll be right there!" I flipped the phone shut, ran out of the restaurant and sprinted to my car. I lived quite a distance away—across town and out in the country. Traffic was heavy and slow and I was in a hurry. I called home, but the line was busy. I called Colin's cell phone, but it was busy, too. I tried both numbers over and over, one after the other. Still busy. In between the dialing, I prayed simple, direct prayers: "Oh, Father, please let her be okay." I must have said that prayer two dozen times. I had no idea why she might be unconscious, but naturally, I was scared to death. Still, I pictured that I would arrive at home and there she would be, sitting in the yard, with the paramedics asking, "Are you sure you're alright?"

Traffic finally began to thin and the home phone rang. Colin answered. Caller ID told him it was me. "Dad, where are you?" he said. My son's voice was anxious.

"I'm on my way home." I mentioned a landmark. "How is she?" I leaned forward in the car seat as if it would speed up the car.

"Dad, they're loading her up in the ambulance. We're going to the hospital. Meet us there." Every word was frantic.

I identified which hospital, and told him I was turning around. "How is she?" I asked again. I expected him to say, "She says she's alright," but he didn't.

"I don't know." I could tell that my son was nervous and scared. So was I. Of course, he could see her. I couldn't.

"Is she conscious?" I asked.

"I don't know. They're giving her oxygen."

"Let me talk to the EMT."

"Okay," he said. I heard his voice away from the phone. "It's my dad. He wants to talk to you."

"Yessir," a busy voice answered quickly.

"How is my wife?" I asked, doing a U-turn. I needed to know something.

"Sir, we're doing everything we can for her. She is stable. We won't know more until we get to the hospital. I have to go."

"Is she conscious?"

"What?" he asked. The din of noise made it hard to hear.

"Is she conscious?" I repeated.

"Not right now, but we'll know more when we get to the hospital. I have to go." He was all business. My heart sank.

"Thank you," I said. "Let me talk to my son." When Colin came back on the line, I gave him some quick instructions and said I would meet him at the emergency room. I hung up the phone and my face yielded to tears. I'd felt this way before. I began to rock in the seat as I drove. I nervously tapped the steering wheel. A dread went over me. "Please, dear God," I begged over and over, "not my sweetheart."

At the hospital, doctors and emergency room staff—friends of ours—worked furiously over her. I began the task of calling family to alert them to what had happened and tell them what little I knew. Eventually, the medical staff stabilized Debbie and moved her to the Critical Care Unit.

Although it took some time to piece the information together, we determined that she suffered a heart attack while working in the front yard, apparently just after she'd spoken with her mom on the phone. Two lawn service workers driving through our neighborhood saw her lying there and mentioned it to our neighbor, Millie, and a friend who was visiting with her. The friend happened to be a registered nurse, and one of the lawn guys was a lifeguard. Both knew CPR. They raced to resuscitate Debbie while Millie called 911. Even though they revived her, she had evidently gone ten to fifteen minutes without oxygen. The odds were against her.

Debbie remained comatose in the hospital for a week before she died on the morning of July 6, just thirty-four days before our thirtieth anniversary. She never regained consciousness—never looked at me, smiled to me, squeezed my hand, kissed my cheek, or spoke a word. Although she battled valiantly, she inevitably, quietly slipped away, and death shoved its way into our lives once more. There it was with its short leash, demanding to have its way with us again. I was in a daze and a state of shock. How suddenly life can change directions and leave you breathlessly stunned. Of course, I knew that already, but still . . . .

Life can throw you a hard curve. Trust me, I know. However, it doesn't have to leave you without hope—hope that you can survive the horrible and dramatic loss that you may face, whatever it is; hope that you can bear the heavy weight of mourning for whatever period of time it may last; hope that you can endure the rest of the day, or the next hour, or even the next minute (when things get that low, and sometimes they do), because others have endured it, and you can, too. Don't stop in the middle of the tunnel; don't quit; don't give up. There is light ahead, at the end of the tunnel.

But before you reach the light, you have to make the journey. Let's take it together.

Chapter 3

Why Me?
(or Why *Not* Me?)

DAVID

The Critical Care Unit was arranged in sort of a U-shape, with the nursing station in the center and individual rooms situated around it. Large plate glass windows allowed the nursing staff to observe inside the rooms.

I sat in Debbie's room next to her bed, my face buried in my hands. She laid there motionless, hooked up to a ventilator, with various lines connected to her arms and chest. A screen above the bed reflected her vital signs, all of which were normal under the circumstances.

A bit earlier that morning, the neurologist who was treating her stopped by on his morning rounds. It was Debbie's first morning there. He examined the pupils of her eyes and performed a couple of other tests. There were a few people in the room with us—Debbie's mother, Kyle and Colin, and perhaps a couple others. We were all hopeful, of course, but I could tell by the doctor's grim demeanor that he was discouraged. He asked me to step outside the room.

He told me that since Debbie had gone without oxygen for such a long period of time, she had sustained a significant brain injury. He was a man of few words, but very compassionate. I was numb as I listened. He asked if I had any questions, and I had two: "What's her prognosis?" I asked. Even though I might not be able to process everything he had explained, I could grasp the answer to that question.

He held his answer for just a second. "Not good," he said succinctly. The answer shook me, but I honestly wasn't surprised. Emotion began to rise within me.

"Okay." I looked through the glass window at Kyle and Colin, a lump rising in my throat. "Doctor," I began, "five years ago we buried our oldest son, their older brother. What do I tell my sons?"

He nodded once to acknowledge that he recognized how important his answer was to me. "Prepare them," he said. "I'm sorry." Tears formed in my eyes while I accepted the news.

The Haunting Question

Later, as I sat alone in her room, I asked myself the haunting question everyone always asks, but especially those who have suffered loss—*why?* Why has death visited my sons and me so much? Why did misfortune come to us *again?*

It wasn't the first time we had asked that question. Five years earlier, after Adam's accident, we struggled with the "why" question. On the Sunday that Adam died, he led the closing prayer at the end of the worship service. I was impressed and proud as I listened to my son. He had matured so much since he moved away to IU. He had grown into a man, both physically and spiritually, and I could tell that as he became less dependent on his parents he had grown more dependent on God.

"And Father," Adam had prayed as he led us that morning, "please be with those who are traveling, not only those who are on their way here, but those who are leaving home to go elsewhere." Adam's words stuck out in my mind. He had the forethought to specifically ask God for his safe travel. Little did we know that he had only eight more hours to live.

Weeks later, struggling through our grief, I could tell Debbie was angry with God. I asked her, point blank, if it was so.

"Yes," she bawled. "It's as if Adam prayed for a safe trip, and God screamed down at him, 'No!'" The word picture was terrifying. I tried to explain, in what was surely a most unsatisfactory way, that God did not kill Adam, a semi-truck did, and that he could not withstand the blunt force of the accident he was in. Eventually, her anger with

God subsided, but I know that Adam's prayer and the "why" question continued to haunt her.

Kyle grappled with similar feelings soon after he arrived at the hospital following Debbie's heart attack. He was in Hartford, Connecticut that day when I called. His cell phone told him that I had called him several times, and I left him a voice mail to phone me as soon as possible. After we finally spoke, I explained what had happened, and the company he worked for graciously flew him immediately to Nashville, where my brother picked him up at the airport, approximately an hour or so away. When Kyle finally got to the hospital at nearly 11:00 P.M., I took him into a separate room and told him what little I knew about his mother's condition. At that point I didn't know much, except that the doctors said the next twelve to twenty-four hours were critical.

Kyle struggled with his words. I could tell he was disturbed. "What's on your mind, son?" I asked him. He stammered and said he didn't know. I then knew the answer, and posed the question: "Are you angry?"

"Yes," he replied, with his head down. I'm sure he thought it would disappoint me.

"Angry with God?" I asked further.

My twenty-three-year-old looked straight at me. "Yes. Dad, this isn't fair. How can this happen again? I want to get married, and I want my mother to be there. I want to have children, and I want my mother to be there. You know what a fantastic grandmother she would be. I don't understand this."

"I know, son," I said, "but God doesn't keep score, and we can't either." At the time, it was all I knew to say to assure him that God was not to blame.

I began to wonder if misfortune would destroy the spiritual foundation we'd tried to instill in our sons. If we experienced more than our fair share of loss and suffering, how could I assure my children, in the face of tragedy, that God is fair and just? Would they confront adversity with dependence on God, the Rock and anchor for our souls, as did King David? "My soul finds rest in God alone: my salvation comes from Him. He alone is my Rock and my salvation; He is my fortress, I will never be shaken" (Ps. 62:1–2). Or would my children reject God as unreliable and unworthy of trust, as did Job's resentful wife in the midst of Job's suffering? *"Curse God and die!"* (Job 2:9). The thought of it worried me.

Job

The story of Job helped me work my way through similar questions several years beforehand. The book begins by introducing us to Job, a blameless and upright man who feared God. He had ten children—seven sons and three daughters—and was a very successful farmer who owned 7,000 sheep, 3,000 camels, 500 teams of oxen, 500 donkeys and a very large number of servants. Scripture describes him as the "greatest man among all the people of the east." He regularly sacrificed burnt offerings for each of his children in the event they may have sinned before God (Job 1:1–5).

Then the scene shifts to God's presence, where the angels approached God, and Satan was with them. God asked Satan where he had been. Satan answered that he had been roaming the earth, going back and forth.

> Then the LORD said to Satan, "Have you considered my servant Job? There is no one on earth like him; he is blameless and upright, a man who fears God and shuns evil."
>
> "Does Job fear God for nothing?" Satan replied. "Have you not put a hedge around him and his household and everything he has? You have blessed the work of his hands so that his flocks and herds are spread throughout the land. But stretch forth your hand and strike everything he has, and surely he will curse you to your face."
>
> The LORD said to Satan, "Very well, then, everything he has is in your hands. But on the man himself do not lay a finger." Then Satan went out from the presence of the LORD.
>
> —Job 1:8–12

The scene then shifts back to earth, when one day disaster strikes. Job received messengers one right after another, telling him the horrible news: a neighboring tribe stole all of his oxen and donkeys and killed his servants; then, all of his sheep and servants were killed by fire from the sky; then, Chaldeans had stolen his camels and killed his servants; and finally, all of his children were feasting at the oldest son's house when a great wind collapsed the house, killing all ten children. Job was devastated.

> At this, Job got up and tore his robe and shaved his head. Then he fell to the ground in worship and said:
>
> "Naked I came from my mother's womb, and naked I will depart.
>
> The LORD gave and the LORD has taken away; may the name of the LORD be praised."
>
> In all this, Job did not sin by charging God with wrongdoing.
> —Job 1:20–22

Scripture does not tell us how much time passed, but once more, the scene shifts, where the angels are again gathered before God, and Satan was with them. Once more, God asked Satan where he'd been, and once more, Satan said he'd been roaming the earth. God again asked:

> "Have you considered my servant Job? There is no one on earth like him; he is blameless and upright, a man who fears God and shuns evil. And he still maintains his integrity, though you incited me against him to ruin him without any reason."
>
> "Skin for skin," Satan replied. "A man will give all he has for his life. But stretch out your hand and strike his flesh and bones, and he will surely curse you to your face."
>
> The LORD said to Satan, "Very well, then, he is in your hands; but you must spare his life."
>
> So Satan went out from the presence of the Lord and afflicted Job with sores from the soles of his feet to the top of his head.
> —Job 2:3–7

Rather than comfort him, Job's wife encouraged him with those four bitter words, to curse God and die. His reaction, however, was both stoic and wise:

> "You are talking like a foolish woman. Shall we accept good
> from God, and not trouble?"
>
> —Job 2:10

Job was then visited by three of his friends who, through much of the rest of the book, struggled to understand why Job had suffered such misfortune. His friends accused him of sin, arguing in simple terms that he must have suffered wrong because he, himself, was a wrongdoer. Job, however, maintained his innocence, and expressed his willingness to argue with God about the fairness of it all. Job asked the "why" question of God: "If I have sinned, what have I done to you, O watcher of men? Why have you made me your target? Have I become a burden to you?" (Job 7:20). Finally, God addressed Job with a series of unanswerable questions, each of which demonstrated the absolute majesty, power, dominion, and sovereignty of God as Creator of everything. Immediately, Job humbly recognized his place.

As the story ends, God blessed Job with prosperity—twice as much wealth as before: 14,000 sheep, 6,000 camels, 1,000 teams of oxen and 1,000 donkeys, plus seven more sons and three more daughters.

> After this, Job lived a hundred and forty years; he saw his
> children and their children to the fourth generation. And so
> he died, old and full of years.
>
> —Job 42:16–17

The story of Job taught me several lessons, three of which I will briefly share now.

First, **Job was one of the finest men on earth**. He was blessed with great wealth and was righteous before God. Yet, he suffered unspeakable tragedy. Lesson: Loss plays no favorites, and is no respecter of persons. It happens to everyone. Neither you nor I have been singled out.

Second (and perhaps this was most important to me), **Job did not suffer misfortune at the hands of God; he suffered at the hands of Satan.** God did not take Job's children, his wealth, or his health. Satan did. God allowed it to happen, but He did not cause it, and there is a major distinction between the two. What does that mean to you and me? Stated bluntly, it is this: God did not kill my Adam or my Debbie or your loved one. God did not cause your hardship or your illness or the breakup of your family or whatever misfortune or loss you are grieving. Satan set all of those things in motion. Lesson: Blame Satan, do not blame God.

Finally, **although the Bible does not describe it all in detail, certainly Job suffered deeply just like me—and you.** We sometimes have the tendency to deify the human characters of the Bible as if they are superhuman, but that is unfair. Scripture describes Job's misery, but doesn't give us the details to questions, like these: When Job received the news of the death of his children, did he run to the scene of the disaster? Did he collect his children's bodies? Did he bury his children himself since he had no servants left to do it? How many days did Job visit their graves and cry in anguish to God over them? He had loved them so much that he regularly sacrificed for each of them on the chance they might have sinned. Can you imagine? How did Job and his wife grieve together? What did they talk about? What did they see in their future with all of their children gone—wiped out in a single storm? In spite of their unimaginable loss, they still served God faithfully. (After all, she did not tell Job to curse God until *after* Satan had struck him the second time, with sores all over his body.)

Do you think Job asked the "why" question after his *first* great trial and *before* the second? Who can know for sure, but it's my guess that he did—it's just not recorded for us. When his wife finally collapsed under the weight of their suffering and encouraged him to quit, do you see Job with clinched teeth and his chin lifted high? Or does he weep in his misery when he says, "Shall we accept good from God and not trouble?" Job was not a man who didn't feel pain; he was just a man who endured pain. Is there a single story of greater tragedy in all of human history? I've never heard it. Do you think Job had bad days? I guarantee it. Yet, Job remained faithful to God, even after misfortune visited him *again*. Lesson: Loss, even great loss, is no reason to turn my back on God. Instead, that is the time I need Him most.

Loss plays no favorites. Do not blame God. Turn toward God, not from Him.

Important lessons, all. Even though I knew the story of Job, I still asked myself the "why" question: Why, indeed, has death visited my sons and me so much? The question burned in my mind as I sat next to Debbie's bed. Suddenly, the painfully obvious answer hit me: *Death visits us all alike; it's just a matter of timing.*

I realized that my family had not experienced death and loss more than any other family, even though I might, for a time, feel like it had. Neither will yours. We will all experience it the same. It's just a matter of when. Truthfully, that realization didn't make me hurt any less at the time, but it did help to remind me that God was not my enemy. He was my friend, my Father. He had not targeted me for some perverse persecution or sent some great punishment on Debbie or me or our family. Instead, He was the Rock and anchor on which I could and had to rely.

I often think of word pictures to help me put things in perspective. One that has been helpful to me is to visualize a great storm and tragedy in life as if I were standing in the middle of a hurricane. The awesome power of the wind and rain is so strong and unrelenting that it seems it will destroy everything in its path. I cannot stand up in it alone. So I cling as tightly as I can to a mighty oak tree—God—to keep me safe, from being blown away, injured, or even killed. The storm still beats on me, but I am moored by the oak and safe from danger. Eventually, the storm subsides and the sky begins to clear. But the clear skies don't last forever. In time, another storm comes, with the same ferocity and pounding strength as the first one before it. What am I to do? Let go of the oak?

Maybe some think that's the thing to do. I don't. The oak will save me from the storms, again and again. I couldn't have made it through my storms without the oak, and for the storms that await me—I hope there are none, but I suspect there will be—I will cling to the oak.

> For who is God besides the LORD?
> And who is the Rock except our God?
>
> —Psalm 18:31

Why *Not* Me?

WILSON

Last night I sat across the table from David as together we talked for four hours at a favorite restaurant (until they closed and told us we had to go home). He talked and I wiped away the tears; I talked and he did the same. I hurt for him and he for me. And, together, we hurt for you. Chances are you didn't pick up this book by accident. Chances are you know something about the pain of which we speak.

There are common threads that run through the ranks of humanity, but none is as common as suffering. We may differ in size, color of skin, likes and dislikes, but there is one thing we share together: each of us knows what it means to hurt. Perhaps that is why suffering has been called the universal language of mankind.

Life is . . . *loss*—the kind of loss that grabs you by the gut, doubles you over, and takes your breath away. Literally. Life is . . . *sorrow*—a sorrow that causes an aching sadness deep within the soul. Life is . . . *pain*—an unbearable, intolerable, silent scream of pain from which there is no escape. I doubt if anyone reading these words is a stranger to these things. If you are, you won't be for long. It scares you, doesn't it? It should.

So, where do you go from here? The divorce is final and there is nothing you can do about it. The abuse really happened and the memory of that day will last a lifetime. The cancer is terminal and no medical marvel will change that fact. The disability is permanent and all the physical therapy in the world will not alter the truth that you will never walk again. The job is really gone. The accident really happened. The casket is really closed . . . and life goes on. Or is supposed to.

But how? What do we do now? How will you make it through this day, much less the next one and the next and . . . It's not a hypothetical question. It is very, very real.

The Storm

In the spring of 1999, an unthinkable thing happened in Nashville, Tennessee. A huge tornado ripped through downtown Music City, moving on to the east and cutting a half-mile-wide swath through the suburbs. One mom reported that she grabbed her child from the clutches of the swirling cloud, and with all her motherly strength, pulled her into the house and together they dove into the basement for safety. The neighborhood of East Nashville was reduced to a natural-disaster area. The next morning, I climbed over trees and through a maze of debris that only hours before represented older homes on a quiet street with people living normal lives—but no more. Residents wandered about that spring morning in housecoats and bedclothes with a faraway look of shock. No one laughed. No one made small talk. Few made eye contact. The aftermath of such a harrowing experience was too great.

The next day was Sunday and I spoke that morning at the worship hour. "On Friday afternoon, some of you crouched in closets, in basements, wherever you could find reasonable shelter and you prayed and made deals with God," I said. "You made the deal that if God would protect you and your family, if you could somehow survive the storm, you would do something for Him." I knew those in the affected area had done exactly that because it is human nature to do so—to appeal to the Almighty when the clouds of chaos come calling and our lives seem to be out of control. At the end of that sermon, seventeen people walked to the front to confess that they had, in fact, done that very thing and they wanted others to know that they intended to hold up their end of the promise.

There was another day in the spring of 1974, when my wife, Julie, huddled in terror in a bathtub while an F-5 monster twister tore through her quiet neighborhood in Xenia, Ohio near Dayton. She could hear it coming and to this day is terrified of tornadoes. And for good reason—the Xenia storm took more than trees and roofs; it took lives. Thirty-two people died, most of them children.

What do I say to storm victims? What advice can I give to hurting people whose lives have come crashing down around them? And they are everywhere. In hospital waiting rooms, funeral homes, nursing homes, and the halls of your local high school where more kids come from hurting homes than we wish to admit. There are survivors all around us whose lonely faces betray the all-too-common fact that life is very, very hard. Sooner or later the storm will come.

So what makes the difference? How are some people able to rise above the most indescribable of tragedies, clear away the debris, and rebuild a shattered life, while others bury themselves in sadness and never learn to live again? Here it is: you may not have a choice about how suffering comes calling, but you do have a choice in how you will respond to that call. We can become bitter or we can become better. And that is more than some cute cliché; it's the truth.

It's a Matter of Choice

I have always wondered why there is more space devoted to the Joseph story in Genesis than to any other—more than to Adam, or Noah, or even Abraham. Joseph, after all, never accomplished the things usually associated with biblical greatness. He never slew a giant, or wrote a line of Scripture, or performed a single miracle. The fact is: Joseph grew up a troubled young man in a dysfunctional home.

So what made him great? In a word . . . *attitude.* Joseph's response to difficult circumstances is what makes his story so special. The man spent much of his life enduring harsh and hateful treatment, and all of it undeserved. But his positive attitude during those long years of tragedy and turmoil offers indisputable proof of his greatness. His faith in God never wavered. *"You meant it for evil,"* he told the very brothers who had sold him into slavery and lied to their father, *"but God meant it for good"* (Gen. 50:20). Joseph couldn't choose his circumstances but he could choose his attitude. And he made the right choice.

It's the same for David—not the biblical giant-slayer son of Jesse, but the Kentucky David who each day comes face-to-face with his own giants.

My friend gets up each morning, showers and shaves, dresses like he's going to a GQ photo shoot (okay, I have to take a shot now and then), and then goes out to meet the demands of another day. How is he able to do that? *Because he chooses to.* It comes down to that. Each day he makes the choice of attitude, demeanor, and mood. Is it easy for him? No. He drives to work near the cemetery where lies the physical remains of his beloved son, next to his mate of nearly thirty years. The hometown where David grew up and spent his entire childhood and adult years presents an ever-present panorama of precious memories.

There is no escape from the split-second pleasantness of those memories, followed by the awful sting of life's reality. It happens to him a hundred times each day. And it happens to you, too.

The answer is not in denial. I worry about those people the most. The answer is not in busyness—that only masks the real problem. The answer is not in drugs, prescribed or otherwise. (I'm not saying that medication has no role in helping some people get back on their feet.) The bottom-line answer, however, lies in an inseparable link to the living Lord.

"How do people make it without God?" I have been asked that question in funeral homes, hospital waiting rooms, and in the living rooms of parents struggling with prodigal children. There was a time when I didn't know the answer to the question, but I do now.

The answer is: *they don't make it!* They deny it. They fake it. They use artificial means to escape it (alcohol, drugs, recreation, busyness, even church-related busyness, and so on), but the one thing they cannot do is face the hardest fact of life: *life is hard.*

This is where the rubber of faith meets the road of reality. If your faith ever stands for something, it must stand for *everything* when life knocks the wind out of your sails. That's why it is essential that you establish personal faith *now* and deepen the roots of conviction in the power and promises of God—because the day will come when the storm winds will blow and you will need those roots to be deep and strong.

Looking back on the days of my own single parenthood, I'm not sure how I made it from one day to the next. Three little ones in tow, spaghetti on the stove, homework to be done, bodies to be cleaned, clothes to be washed and dried, housework to be done, night after night after night. It's enough work for two people—that's how God designed it. I think often about the story of the footprints in the sand. I can't quote it but I'll never forget the line when the author discovers only one set of prints along the sandy shoreline. Thinking God had abandoned him in the midst of the storm, he cries out in desperation as to why God would allow him to walk alone. *"Dear child,"* says the Father, *"it was then that I carried you."* I think there were days and nights that He carried me. Looking back on it now, I'm sure of it.

Little Eyes Are Watching

Influence is a powerful thing and few of us ever realize the power of one. A few hours north of our home is Mammoth Cave National Park. Years ago it, along with Niagara Falls, was a premier honeymoon destination but that was before all the bigger and better (?) man-made resorts came along. I still have a fondness for Mammoth and go back now and again with the same kid-like excitement I had years ago. At one point on most tours, the park ranger gathers the tour group together in a tight circle and then turns out all the lights. Darkness. Not kind-of, sort-of darkness, but total and complete blackness. (One of my kids once wore a pair of sneakers with the red lights that blinked when he walked which, as you might guess, totally killed the effect!) The ranger then lights a single match and it sets off a glow that fills the room. Yes, there is power in one light.

My friend, *you are that light.* I had to keep going in front of my kids because I knew they were watching. And something amazing was happening while they were watching. Their little minds were depositing away information that would be stored for years to come in a marvelous invention of God called a "memory bank." One day my kids will need to make a withdrawal from what they have saved because one day my kids will go through hard times. And whether or not they survive the storm will depend a great deal on whether or not they have made enough faith deposits. Circumstances may be different for them, but the pain will be all too common. I hope that when they face the whirling clouds of upheaval they will then remember what their daddy did. And I want them to know that if I could do it, they can, too.

The last thing David said to me last night as I drove him back to his car may be the most memorable thing of our four-hour conversation. "I have to be an example for my sons." He's right. Kyle and Colin may be adult children but they are still his children and he their father. The mantle of parenthood never goes away. David is showing his sons that his faith is real because one day they, too, will be faced with difficulties and will need to make a withdrawal from the deposits he has helped them make. And they will remember . . . They will remember that Dad faced the crucible of hard times and did so with confident faith.

Parents leave behind a lot of things for their children. Some leave gifts of monetary inheritance, real estate, meaningful mementos, etc., while others leave behind something of much greater value. Wise are the parents who leave behind the greatest gift of all—the gift of strong faith and determined trust in the God they serve.

To face difficult circumstances outside of our control and beyond our choice does not make us unique. In fact, it is the one thing each of us has in common. It's how we respond to them that sets us apart.

"I have to be an example for my sons."

I drove home with those words etched upon my mind.

Chapter 4

Everyone Has a Story

WILSON

A few years ago I watched as our forty-third president was sworn into office for his second term. The cold and gray January sky gave way to bright sunshine as dignitaries and the famous found their seats as the noon hour approached. Regardless of political persuasion, America's elected leaders gather every four years on this day and our nation celebrates the smooth transition of power. It is truly a remarkable occasion of pageantry, and a strong reminder of our democracy and freedom.

But in the end, they too are just people. Strip away the pomp and circumstance, the ruffles and flourishes, the black ties and fur coats (and with this president from the dusty streets of tiny Crawford, Texas, a few fancy cowboy boots), and you will find men and women who hurt just like the rest of us. The Chief Justice of these United States, the Honorable William H. Rehnquist who courageously administered the oath of office, has since lost his battle with cancer. Former President Gerald Ford, like Rehnquist, has since passed on. Presidents Carter and Bush show signs of old age. Even the boyish look of President Clinton has faded as scandal and time have left their marks. President Reagan is with us no more as Alzheimer's and age finally took their toll. And over his eight years, President Bush and First Lady Laura Bush faced the difficult challenge of not only managing the country's affairs but of responding to the demands of raising independently-minded twin daughters (the latter probably kept the former in perspective).

Pain plays no favorites, not even among the rich and powerful in Washington, D.C. Nor does it play favorites among common folk like us. Everyone, I have learned, has a story . . .

⚬⚬⚬

Marilyn

I met Marilyn in the fall of 2006 in Lawrenceburg, Tennessee—a quiet rural community in the southern and central part of the state, known mostly for being home to former Senator and current TV and film star, Fred Thompson. After I spoke one evening about the trials and triumphs of Job, this thirty-something mother of three waited until most of the crowd had gone home and then approached me in the foyer with her story. "I am a breast cancer survivor," she said. She went on to relate that when she was stricken with the disease, she gathered her wits along with her faith and prayed that God's will be accomplished in her life. If it were His will that she lose her battle only to go home to Him, then she would find the faith to accept that. On the other hand, if it were His will for her to survive and linger longer with family and friends, she would engage the battle and fight with every ounce of energy she had. Marilyn fought hard, and by God's grace, she conquered the enemy.

But she wasn't finished.

To celebrate her recovery, she set her heart to climb a mountain and thank God for His strength. But not just any mountain . . . Marilyn's mountain climb would take her outside the United States and all the way to Tanzania where she set her sights on 19,340-foot Mt. Kilimanjaro—Africa's highest peak.

She trained for over a year. When the time was right and she was ready, the team left base camp and began the ascent. "Only two in our climb team made it to the summit," she explained, "and I was one of them." "And when I finally made it," she said, "I sank to my knees and thanked God for His blessings." Speaking with a voice of determination and thankfulness, she concluded, "I have gone from the valley of the shadow of death to standing on top of the world. And God has been with me in BOTH places." She went on, "I promised that I would praise Him, not only in the lowest valleys of my life, but from the highest hill I could climb." And she did.

Marilyn has a story.

Brenda

No one knows. Although Brenda is a dedicated Christian wife and mother, she harbors a double secret—her husband's agnosticism and alcoholism. Brenda is determined to exemplify the character of 1 Peter 3:1 and win her husband "without a word" by the godly example of her consistent and faithful life. She may succeed or she may not. But each day she tries with only the strength that God supplies. Each day the burden is there and some days it seems beyond bearable as she seeks to maintain her own faith as well as work to influence her son for good. It's not easy but she is determined.

Brenda has a story.

Sandy

I'll let Sandy tell you in her own words . . .

We were married in 1991 and he was completely in love with me and I with him. At least that's what I thought. I was wrong. I also thought that I knew him. I was wrong about that, too. On our honeymoon and in a foreign country, he began yelling at me when I could not quickly locate directions on a map—"You stupid MORON, you can't even read a map!" I began to sob. Thus began our married life. It didn't get any better.

During my pregnancies, he was disinterested, overworked me, screamed if the work piles he gave me during the day were not finished on time, belittled me for having brought no income into the family, and reminded me that without him I would be NOTHING. The years took their toll and I battled depression. By the time our third child was born, he was hardly ever at home and I seldom went out. My husband kept hurting me and I pleaded with him to stop. The depression deepened and I found myself begging God to take my life. I did not want to live anymore. I remember going for walks in the rain, yet never feeling wet. Was it me? Was I unlovable? What was wrong with me? Maybe God didn't even love me . . .

I suffered terribly. I prayed daily. I never let go of God, but I was certainly not completely trusting. Over time I realized that by begging to die, that meant my children would be left to him and by now his verbal abuses were often directed to them as well. I could not bear that thought. And that's when I began to pray that *he* would die . . .

As I grew in my relationship to God, I began to make changes. I would take long walks and talk to the Lord about the pain. I determined to be the best mother I could be and to compliment my husband often. At first that was hard to do because I was so embittered against him, but eventually it became easier. He even began to praise me in between his outbursts. I began to see how God really loved and cared about me. I began to count my blessings instead of my problems. I was rich in friendships and by now had four beautiful children. God had been very good to me . . .

My husband didn't deserve my kindness and submission, but God did. I would do it for Him. I had seen my sisters give up their marriages and had seen the terrible pain in the faces of their children. I realized what a fallacy divorce really is. I was thankful that even in my stubborn state, I had clung to the teaching of Scripture. It became apparent to me that even though God's ways were often hard, man's ways were even harder. My sisters who left their husbands were not happier and neither were their children.

The nasty outbursts continued, breaking open the scars each time—and each time I prayed that God would help me to love him. I was beginning to succeed.

It was a typical Saturday morning that found me lying in bed enjoying a few cherished moments of peaceful sleep when I heard him yell. At first I thought he was yelling at the boys but the large CRASH that followed got my attention. I ran to the living room and found him making strange sounds while banging his head repeatedly on the floor while his body twitched uncontrollably. His color was not good. I flew to him and began calling his name. I called 911 . . .

Tests revealed that he had a massive tumor on the left side of his brain which was beginning to put pressure on his skull. It was so large and intertwined with his brain that surgery was not an option. I was shocked. Was this a punishment from God for having prayed that he would die? Was this my fault? Did God wait until I realized I loved him to take him from me?

Four long months passed while I stayed at his side. During this time he became more violent than ever. I remember praying, 'God, please, have mercy on us!' How was I ever going to take care of him? I had four little ones at home . . . Where would I find the strength? Finally, at 6:30 in the morning I closed my eyes and slept. I awoke to a nurse checking for vital signs—and that's when I saw that he was not breathing. He was bluish gray and strangely still. When I realized that he was dead, I began to shake from head to foot . . . I felt responsible. I felt that it was my fault. I felt that everyone would blame me for his death. I sobbed and sobbed.

Later that day I had to tell my children and each one reacted differently. My own grief was just as complicated. Part of me felt relief that he was gone. He had been so cruel to the children, and to me. The last few months had been worse than ever. Yet he was my husband and I depended upon him. What would happen to us? How could I be both mother and father? Will the children grow up blaming God? Somehow I got through the wake and the funeral. I did not cry. I was too numb to cry. I craved to be alone, yet I was thankful for all those who reached out to me.

During all those years that my husband was alive and abusive, I learned to play a little game I called "Rainbow Seeking." Basically, it was looking for the good in every bad situation. I felt that a rainbow parallels our struggles: 1) it must be raining in front of you (you must be facing a dark time), and 2) the sun must be shining in back of you (the SON is behind you all the way). These thoughts brought me great comfort and I found that there was always a rainbow in the darkest of my times. Looking for those pieces of hope reminded me that God was always there helping me; that He had never forsaken me. Isaiah 41:10–13 was my greatest source of comfort. Any time I would feel sad, I would read these verses again and again and remember that God's love is very real, very strong, and very near.

> Do not fear, for I am with you;
> Do not anxiously look about you,
> for I am your God.
> I will strengthen you, surely I will help you.
> Surely I will uphold you with My righteous right hand.
> Behold, all those who are angered at you
> will be shamed and dishonored;
> Those who contend with you will be as nothing, and will perish.
> You will seek those who quarrel with you, but will not find them,
> Those who war with you will be as nothing . . .
> For I am the Lord your God, who upholds your right hand,
> Who says to you, "Do not fear, I will help you."

Sandy has a story.

Reggie and Janice

I've known Reggie and Janice all my life along with their children, Kim and Mark. Kim and I grew up together in Louisville and although we were never extremely close, we remained friends. That friendship solidified in the mid-1980s when I stayed in the home of Kim and her husband, Gary, while preaching for the small church in Caribou,

Maine—an outpost from nowhere but home to Loring Air Base, a SAC Base of Operations for B-52s and where Gary was stationed. It was a wonderful week.

Kim passed away a few years ago from her battle with cancer and her parents faced the unnatural experience of burying their daughter. If that were not enough, son Mark was involved in an automobile accident a couple years ago, never fully recovered, and eventually joined his sister in death. Today Reggie and Janice face each day together but alone—bereft of both their children.

"How do you cope?" I asked Reggie while we ate together at a Louisville area restaurant on a cold November day. "It's the hardest thing I've ever done," he said. He continued, "I've heard people say you have to take it a day at a time . . . but in our case it's more like one minute at a time." Even though Mark's death had occurred a couple months previous, this was the first time either Reggie or Janice had gone out individually—Reggie with several preacher-friends and Janice on a lunch date with the ladies from church. "It will be good for her," he noted. "She needed to get out." He went on to speak of the depth of their grief and told of how he sought to be strong for her until . . . until she went to bathe and that's when he would step into the backyard and, in his own words, "cry like a baby."

Reggie and Janice are facing a hurt that won't go away. Ever. It's minute by minute for them. They have a story.

⸙

Rickie

November 1, 1986 will be a day that Rickie will never forget. It was a cold and overcast day along the Rio Grande near Del Rio, Texas. Rickie and five other friends put out in the water in three small aluminum boats ready for a day of fishing near the Amisted Dam. Unknown to them, the flow of water being released from the huge dam that day was tremendous and had they known of the danger, they would not have been there.

One mile below the dam they approached one of the smaller weir dams—an outflow of concrete that, when the runoff is high, as it was that day, would create what locals called a "boil"—a swirl of water that could easily flip a boat. Before anyone knew what had happened, the lead boat was caught in the boil, flipping the boat and throwing the two occupants overboard. The force of the water in such boils was known to be strong enough to turn railroad ties into splinters. Vernon was gone immediately. His body would be recovered later that day. Bill, a United States Border Patrol agent, was in the fight for his life but to no avail. The boil took him down and it would be the next day before they would locate his body.

When the second boat came to the rescue, it too was caught in the boil and both Rickie and Robert were likewise tossed into the swirling waters. Rickie tells what happened. "Robert and I struggled with every ounce of energy we had. Somehow he broke free but I was caught. The water kept pushing me up and down and I knew that the next time it took me down would be my last." With tears welling in his eyes, he continued, "I thought about Jody and the kids—who were nine and seven at the time. And I thought about getting ready to meet the Lord. I had already seen what had happened to Vernon and Bill and I knew that this was it." He is still unsure what happened next but he remembers swimming with all his might when someone reached out and pulled him into the third boat, thus saving his life. Amazingly Robert had also survived even though both men suffered from hypothermia.

Some twenty-two years later, it is still hard for Rickie to talk about the events of that day. He lost two of his dearest friends, almost another, and nearly his own life. It is an event that he lives and relives again and again. It never goes away.

Rickie has a story.

Pap

Mike and Janice live on a picturesque ranch in the Piney Woods of East Texas near Lufkin. Next to their home was the residence of their daughter and son-in-law, Jennifer and Brent, along with their grandchildren Mikah (four) and Luke (two). Never has a grandfather been crazier about his grandkids than was Pap. He loved lifting them into the cab of his big John Deere and taking them for rides around the ranch. Theirs was a special bond.

Mike never saw him on that fateful February day. When little Luke heard Pap start the big tractor, he bolted from the house and ran toward his grandfather. Mike positioned the tractor into place to secure a roll of hay and once affixed, pulled out and through the gate toward the pasture. Mikah who had followed her little brother outside, saw the accident and ran back inside yelling for her mother and telling her that Luke was hurt and bleeding. Jennifer, her heart beating wildly, dropped what she was doing and ran from the house where . . . where she came upon Luke's lifeless body lying on the ground. She knelt over her son and realized he was gone.

No one knows exactly what happened although the family speculates that Luke tried to climb up the big tractor and fell off or perhaps he was obscured by one of the huge tires. In the meantime, the whole scene was unknown to Mike who had proceeded toward the pasture. Only when he saw the commotion in the yard did he realize that something was wrong. He raced back to find Jennifer and Luke and only then did it begin to dawn on him what had happened.

Mike lives each day with the realization of the accident. Yet it was Mike's strength of faith that led his family through the crisis. The next Sunday, Mike, an elder of the church, walked with his family into worship services; Mike in the lead. And by so doing, Mike led not only his family, but also an entire congregation; to a greater understanding about faith and trust even in things you don't understand.

"I don't question, 'Why?'" says Mike. "The 'Why?' is beyond my understanding." And then he adds, "But I have learned that when the hours are darkest, God's grace is the greatest."

Brent and Jennifer have since left the ranch, and in addition to Mikah, God has blessed them with a little girl, Claire, and two beloved sons, Paul and Levi. To this day, however, when you ask them how many children they have, they will smile and say, "Five. We have five children . . ." Luke continues to live—in the Lord's presence and in their hearts. They will tell you that they have learned to live with joy in the midst of sorrow.

Mike and Janice still live on the ranch. Their home is next to a beautiful flower garden built as a memorial to their beloved grandson. Pap was eventually able to get back on his tractor again and oversee his fields but more than that Pap was able to oversee the needs of his family—physically and spiritually—and help them be being a living example of how a shepherd handles grief. He is an inspiration to everyone who knows him.

Brent and Jennifer have a story. So does Janice and so does Pap.

Debbie

Debbie was on the receiving end of abuse and an unfaithful mate. When I first met her, she described the pain of divorce as "a Civil War triage where your limb is amputated without anesthesia." If that were not enough, one year later her beloved son, Gabriel, was fatally struck down in an accident on the way to school. There are no words to describe the intensity of her pain. Debbie did take solace, however, in the knowledge that she had raised a great young Christian man who just days before had declined an invitation to attend a party where his friends were drinking, only to find himself on the receiving end of peer insults. Days later those same friends walked by his casket and each of them dropped in a note of apology.

Debbie has a story.

David

My friend and co-author has a story that you have already read. I remember a September day in 2003 when David and I, along with half a dozen other men, were hiking in the backcountry of Montana's Glacier National Park near the border with British Columbia. We had put a couple miles behind us on what was a beautiful fall day in the Rockies, when David began to speak of his beloved son, Adam. At some point along the rugged trail, he could go no further. He stopped and dropped his pack and wept quietly. We all stopped. One by one the sound of "thud" could be heard as all of our backpacks hit the ground while a group of grown men shared a few quiet moments of compassion with our hurting friend. Yes, men cry, too. After a time, we wiped our eyes, strapped on our packs, and continued the silent journey. Little did David know then that a year later death would invade his home again.

David has a story.

Julie

She came into a ready-made family (Dr. Phil would ask, "Girl, what were you thinkin'?") She, however, brought help and healing to a broken home and gave my children the emotional bond of a mother's love that had been missing for a long time. Like Debbie above, she will write her own chapter, but I dare say that anyone who has ever assumed the role of a stepparent—giving birth to children in the heart and not the womb—each of them has a story.

How many of us are there?

"Preach to broken hearts, there is one in every pew." I don't know who said that but they are wrong. They are wrong not because of the brokenness but because of the number. The truth is—there is *more* than one in every pew. Sometimes I think it is everyone on the pew!

The trouble is that we all look so nice and normal. On any given Sunday we parade into church wearing our best suits and smiles. We are preachers and elders and their wives, deacons and song leaders, Bible class teachers and moms and dads—all joyously singing, "If the skies above you are gray, you are feeling so blue . . ." And all the while we sing, we think we are the only ones struggling and barely making it, the only ones suffering, the only ones really feeling *"so blue."* But I know better. I know better because I know that . . . *everyone has a story* of hurt and hardship. Everyone.

So let's quit pretending. Let's quit pretending as if we have all the answers to all the questions. Let's quit pretending that we don't hurt and suffer and cry. Let's quit pretending that we never doubt, or worry, or question, or get angry, or wander about confused. It's time to face the reality of our suffering and . . . it's time to reach out to one another. *"Rejoice with those who rejoice, and weep with those who weep."*

My friend, you are not alone. Think about that the next time you are tempted to feel as if you are the only one. Although your grief is very personal and very real, you are not alone in the daily struggle. There are countless others facing the same uphill climb. Don't despair, because . . . *everyone has a story.*

Note: Some names have been changed in this chapter out of respect for privacy.

Chapter 5

When the Laughter Stops

DAVID

After Adam's accident, it was nearly midnight when we got home from the hospital. We walked into our house, but it felt different. It was the same den and same furniture where Adam had napped only hours before, but it was forever changed. It wasn't a happy place anymore. I sat on a hassock and stared at the floor into nothingness—stunned, expressionless, empty—just a shell. I could change nothing: not the speed of Adam's car; not that second of inattention; not the moment of the collision; not his death; nothing. The irreversibility of it all was devastating.

I wanted to reach into the past and change even the slightest thing. If Adam had left our house just *two seconds* later, would that have been enough? If he had been caught by just one traffic light, would that have been enough? If he had spent a moment longer at the gasoline station, would that have been enough? "What ifs?" haunt the mind of a grieving parent, even though they do no good. His death sent me reeling. The entire world had spun out of control. I had no power over anything. I've never felt so helpless in all my life. That is, until I sat in Debbie's hospital room at Vanderbilt University Medical Center the afternoon before she died.

The chief of the neurology department had met with me, Kyle, and Colin, and explained in detail the nature of Debbie's condition, why she wasn't reacting to some of the simple neurological tests he and the nursing staff had performed, and how he expected her brain to react physiologically in the next few hours to the next few days. He patiently answered every question. Still, the news was dreadful. She suffered from brain anoxia—lack of oxygen to the brain—and once the damage had been done, it could not be reversed. Dead brain cells do not and cannot regenerate. In addition, the trauma to her brain from oxygen deprivation was causing her brain to swell and that, in turn, would eventually cause her death.

After I shared our conversation with Debbie's family, we made the heart-wrenching decision that when the time came for her to go, we would let her go. I returned to her hospital room and sat by her bed. I looked at her, lying there so peacefully, but altogether unable to respond to me or doctors or even pain or light. I spoke to her briefly, hoping against hope that she would answer, but of course, she didn't. That's when I felt so helpless. I didn't know when she would die, but I knew it would be soon. A week before, we were planning a thir-tieth wedding anniversary trip to Europe; we intended to grow old together. Now, the hours I had left with her were numbered. There was nothing—absolutely nothing—I could do to change it. I walked out of her room, approached one of her doctors standing at the nurses' station, and signed a DNR order—"Do Not Resuscitate." I felt like I'd been punched; I could hardly breathe. I walked down the hall to my family, my chin on my chest, in a state of shock—a shell like I'd felt five years before sitting in my den. I had just signed an order to let my wife, my sons' mother and my best friend, die.

How could our world change so dramatically so quickly? In the ring of a cell phone call, everything suddenly changed and our plans were meaningless. Instead of traveling across the Atlantic to visit the Old World, I traveled across town to visit the cemetery; instead of buying my wife lunch in a Paris café, I bought flowers to place at her grave.

I recalled then what I had realized five years before—control over events in your life is an illusion. We are especially reminded of it when life spins out of control. Truthfully, however, we're just as helpless when things go well as when things go bad. We just remember it when things go bad and we want to change the course of events. I had no control over my world *before* Adam's accident, or Debbie's heart attack. It just seemed like I did. Horrible, unforeseen events intervened and reminded me that I really had no control at all.

The experience reminds me what we all know but rarely think about: the world is fragile and unpredictable. It is subject to radically sudden and permanent changes in the blink of an eye, all of which (except those we personally set in motion) are beyond our individual command. We cope with that frightening realization by reasoning that "it may happen to someone else, but it won't happen to me." Oh, yeah? How many hurting "someone else's" are out there? We work in every town; we live on every street; we shop in every store. And "someone else" joins our ranks every day, every hour, every minute. For me, it happened in the moment of an auto accident on I-65 and a heart attack in the front yard of my home. For you, it's happened with a death, divorce, life-threatening disease, or some other misfortune or loss that has shaken your world off its foundation. Whatever the case, we all—all of us—face the random assault of tragedy.

The wise man, Solomon, poetically described how abruptly life can change in Ecclesiastes 9:11–12:

> I have seen something else under the sun:
> The race is not to the swift or the battle to the strong, nor
> does food come to the wise or wealth to the brilliant or favor
> to the learned; but time and chance happen to them all.
>
> Moreover, no man knows when his hour will come:
> As fish are caught in a cruel net, or birds are taken in a snare,
> so men are trapped by evil times that fall unexpectedly upon
> them.

For weeks after Adam's accident, I couldn't do *anything* without his death on my mind. The horror of it was constantly present. As if I were holding my fist against my face between my eyes, I could not see, feel, or do anything, literally, without noticing it. It was impossible to avoid, there all the time. When I went to bed, I hated to close my eyes because the unimaginable nightmare of his death flooded my mind. When I woke up in the morning, it jolted me into the day. Even when I interacted with others, it consumed my thoughts. I specifically recall standing in the checkout line at a convenience store, and feeling as if it were written all over me, like I had a sign around my neck that blared, "My son just died!" I was constantly distracted. Work was difficult. I could not escape it.

A friend gave me a book for the grief-stricken, highlighting thirty poignant daily Psalms. It was the first book I read after Adam's death (besides excerpts I chose from the Bible), and it helped to focus my mind with the spiritual perspective of David, the psalmist. David's psalms reminded me that I wasn't the first to go down this path—others had been there and survived. "How long, O Lord?" he wrote, "Will You forget me forever? How long will You hide Your face from me? How long must I wrestle with my thoughts and every day have sorrow in my heart?" (Ps. 13:1–2). David wrote heart-wrenching words. He'd been here before. He hurt the way I hurt, and felt the way I felt. And he knew the way out of it. That began to lift my hope to just a little above the hopeless line.

Wherever I went, friends consoled me—which was a wonderful blessing—and even though I thanked them for their sympathy and prayers (and I *was* thankful for them), inside I was completely and utterly vacant. Life felt *so* empty. I couldn't laugh. I even found it hard to smile—literally. Humor was difficult for me to find in the depth of my sorrow. I felt stripped of meaning and purpose, of even the spirit to live. I know Debbie did, too. If you've lost a child, you know what I mean. It was the deepest valley.

Job had been where I was, and he expressed how I felt:

- *Why did I not perish at birth, and die as I came from the womb?* (Job 3:11).

- *Or why was I not hidden in the ground like a stillborn child, like an infant who never saw the light of day?* (Job 3:16).

- *What I feared has come upon me; what I dreaded has happened to me. I have no peace, no quietness; I have no rest, but only turmoil* (Job 3:25–26).

- *Why then did You bring me out of the womb? I wish I had died before any eye saw me. If only I had never come into being, or had been carried straight from the womb to the grave!* (Job 10:18–19).

If you just experienced loss, you may be where I was. When you feel so helpless, where do you turn for help? When your world is shaken to its very core and spins out of control—so much that you wish you hadn't been born—what should you do? Cling to the Lord. Hold on and don't ever let go. He is steady and firm, and the only place to find stability.

Scripture reverberates with encouragement that God is in charge, that He is unchanging and reliable, even when our entire world feels so unsteady and everything around us seems so frail. Read these simple passages slowly; meditate on their deep meaning.

- God is not a man, that He should lie, nor a son of man, that He should change His mind. Does He speak and then not act? Does He promise and not fulfill? (Num. 23:19).

- "Never will I leave you; never will I forsake you" (Deut. 31:6; Heb. 13:5).

- Your word, O Lord, is eternal; it stands firm in the heavens. Your faithfulness continues through all generations; You established the earth and it endures (Ps. 119:89–90).

- Do you not know? Have you not heard? The Lord is the everlasting God, the Creator of the ends of the earth. He will not grow tired or weary, and His understanding no one can fathom (Isa. 40:28).

- "I the Lord do not change" (Mal. 3:6).

- We have this hope [of eternal salvation] as an anchor for the soul, firm and secure (Heb. 6:19).

- Jesus Christ is the same yesterday, today and forever (Heb. 13:8).

Regardless of what's happened in my life (or in yours), Scripture reminds us that God is still in charge—or as my friend Kevin Morrow puts it, He is still on the throne. Truthfully, the only thing that changed for me was that I lost the illusion I was in control. In fact, I was never in control in the first place. I needed to revisit my perspective.

Let me illustrate it this way. In the movie *The Perfect Storm*, a conflagration of three storm fronts in the northern Atlantic traps a small fishing boat that has traveled too far out to sea. As the storm gathers over the ocean, satellite photos show the storm form into its familiar swirl, but the storm is so huge the fishing boat cannot escape. In one of the closing scenes of the movie, the small boat, caught in the middle of the monstrous storm, hopelessly fights wave after crushing wave. The gallant crew tries to save the boat, but it is no match for the onslaught of water. Towering, unyielding hundred-foot waves easily overpower the boat, and literally swallow her up into the ocean.

How does perspective affect events? If I imagine myself in the boat in the center of the storm, I see and feel the battering waves that surround me, and I suffer in first person the imminent, heart-wrenching panic from the catastrophic events over which I have no control. However, if I step away mentally and picture the same events from a different perspective—imagine them as though I were watching from a great distance, like from the surface of the moon—I see something altogether different. The whirling form of the storm may briefly appear over the northern Atlantic, but I cannot see a boat or even hundred-foot waves. Instead, the immediate details of that specific event dissolve into a larger view of something greater: the peaceful blue sphere of our planet.

Does changing perspective change the event? No. Does it stop the boat from sinking or change the catastrophe in the center of the storm? Of course not. Should I detach myself and ignore the things happening around me? No, not even if I could. But when the time comes to heal, understanding change of perspective alters my view of the storm and helps me see that there is more going on than just my storm. It helps me see over and past the blinding waves of sorrow I face, so that the acute sense of helplessness and panic does not destroy me. It reminds me that somewhere, beyond my spot in the ocean, there is peace, and that even though my world seems upside down, it won't stay that way. It gives me a longer and larger view of the events of life—not the same as, but more akin to, God's eternal view. It reminds me that I *can't* control what happens, but I *can* control how I react to what happens.

For example, viewing the stories of Job and Joseph from the *end* of their lives gives us a longer perspective of the events that turned their worlds upside down. If they had given up on the Lord in the middle of their crises, who can say their stories would have ended the same?

Do not misunderstand: refocusing perspective is not detachment from reality or an immediate salve for grief, sorrow, hurt, or despair. But when you remind yourself that God is in control, your sense of hopelessness will eventually heal into hope.

Truthfully, following Adam's death I wasn't immediately able to consider my perspective to help me begin to heal because the pain and horror of the event were too immense. A kind and wise friend shared words of perspective with me, but the weight of Adam's loss was so overwhelming that I couldn't change my view. My feet were firmly nailed to the horror of it all. I couldn't move or escape from it, and I wasn't able to change perspective—not then. Although I understood what I needed to do intellectually, it probably took me a couple of years to completely process. Changing my perspective gave me a different way to view Adam's death—and life. It helped me move from wrenching over his death and the horrible loss to an attitude of thankfulness for the years I was blessed to have him. Instead of fretting about the life I had without him, I focused on the life I had with him. Truthfully, God blessed me with Adam for twenty-one years. Shouldn't I have been thankful?

When Debbie lay in the hospital in a coma, my friend, Steve Thornton, helped to console me and quietly put her tragedy in perspective this way: He asked, "I know this is not what you expected, but when you met and were about to get married, if the Lord had said to you, 'I will let you have her, but you can only have her for thirty years,' what would you have said?" I knew what he was asking. I replied, "I would have said, 'Yes, of course, I want whatever time I can have.'" My friend said, "Well, you've had it." His question required me to view the events from a different perspective, with thanksgiving for the time I'd had. I wasn't being cheated; I had been blessed. Of course, the wound did not heal immediately, but learning to view the events with a different perspective helped prepare my mind to begin the healing process.

When the infant son of King David and Bathsheba died, David instructed all grieving parents who follow him with his memorable statement, "I will go to him, but he will not return to me" (2 Sam. 12:23). Even though our hearts break and ache over the loss of our children or anyone else in our lives, David correctly puts it all into perspective, and after the blunt force of loss begins to subside, David's reminder helps.

A psalm that I read perhaps more than any other, and one I've shared with many in the same position, is Psalm 34:17–19:

> The righteous cry out, and the Lord hears them; He delivers them from all their trouble.
>
> The Lord is close to the brokenhearted and saves those who are crushed in spirit.
>
> A righteous man may have many troubles, but the Lord delivers him from them all.

After Adam and Debbie died, I read that passage every day. It assured me that the Lord heard every prayer I cried to Him; that He would not leave me hurting forever, and that He would heal my heart and lift the weight of grief from me. It renewed my confidence that I wasn't just one of many millions who approached Him each day, but that He noticed *me*; that He wanted to ease *my* suffering; and He would deliver *me* from the awful hurt I carried.

The passage of scripture that gave me the greatest comfort of all was Matthew 11:28–30. Even when I read it now, it brings a lump to my throat.

> Come to Me, all you who are weary and burdened, and I will give you rest. Take My yoke upon you and learn from Me, for I am gentle and humble in heart, and you will find rest for your souls. For My yoke is easy and My burden is light.

Some students of the Bible may argue that Jesus' words are directed to those burdened with sin, and I do not disagree. But doesn't He say more than that? Listen to the words of the Lord. The Christ of heaven says to His listeners and to each of us, "Come to Me!" To those of us who are tired and want to give up from the heavy load and emotional weariness of life, He says, "Come to Me!" To those of us who bear the burden of loss or divorce or disease, He says, "Come to Me!" We may be burdened with sin—all of us are—but I read Jesus' words as His personal plea from heaven to lay down the weight and worry and pain of life, and give it all to Him. He *does* lift burdens; He *does* carry the heavy weight of life's cares; and when you're too weak and fragile to go any further, He will carry you, too.

But that's not all. There was something else I had to remind myself—another perspective I needed to remember: Adam's and Debbie's deaths were not the end of things for them. My loss was their gain. They were both faithful Christians. God's promise to deliver from trouble is not limited to our existence in this lifetime. Rather, more importantly, He saves us in the after-lifetime. It was confidence in that very principle that motivated the apostle Paul to be the great servant that he was (2 Cor. 4:16–18), and he wanted to pass that same confidence in immortality to others, including us, to encourage us and lift us, even in the worst of times.

In 1 Thessalonians 4:13–18, Paul told the Christians at Thessalonica that he did not want them "to grieve like the rest of men, who have no hope." Instead, he described the Lord's powerful return, and said, "Encourage each other with these words." If I am to take Paul's words to heart, I will focus on my expectation of Christ's return and my hope for immortality for those I love.

The writer of the letter to the Hebrews expresses the same kind of message and hope for resurrection:

> Since the children have flesh and blood, He [Christ] too shared in their humanity so that by His death He might destroy him who holds the power of death—the devil—and free those who all their lives were held in slavery by their fear of death.
>
> —Hebrews 2:14–15

God wants us to know that there is no reason to fear death—or to unreasonably grieve about those who have died! That reason is resurrection. The rationale for this is varied, but here's one simple reminder to constantly repeat when you need a lift:

> He will wipe every tear from their eyes. There will be no more death or mourning or crying or pain, for the old order of things has passed away.
>
> —Revelation 21:4

If I want to heal from grief—if *you* want to heal from grief—we must revisit God's promise of resurrection over and over. If you're tired and weary from the load and pain of this fragile world, then you must lay it all down at the feet of Jesus. If you're not able to climb out of the awful pit of grief, then you need to increase your faith in His promises. How did God deliver Jesus from the trouble He faced at Calvary? The answer is the empty tomb! (Heb. 12:2). That's the promise that awaits Christians, and the foundation rock upon which to begin to heal.

When I fought my daily battles with grief, I frequently read the story of the rich man and Lazarus (Luke 16:19–31). It helped me to visualize the safety in which the Lord kept Adam and Debbie—and, honestly, the safety that awaits me. Perhaps like many have done, I asked myself whether I would bring them back if it were within my power to do so. How could I do it? How selfish for me to deprive them of such a great reward just for my temporary solace. Make no mistake: faith and confidence in God's promises are tested in the turmoil of sorrow, but to abandon Him is to abandon the only thing that will save you from complete misery.

Changing my perspective about life and loss helped me. The concepts were not new. I understood them long before Adam or Debbie died. The challenge—the uphill challenge—was to apply them in the depth of despair. I had to transform intellectual concepts that are easy to talk about into concrete, life rules to help me get by. I learned through my experiences, and I look back on them now with great confidence in God's ability to deliver me and my family, not only from the pain of life, but also from the pain of death—from life into glory.

Read on. Wilson will explain how.

WILSON

The Laughter Stops but the "Joy" Doesn't

When Peter and James penned their inspired accounts, both wrote to Christians who were all too familiar with the subject of suffering. Peter wrote his first letter "to those who reside as aliens, scattered throughout . . ." (1:1) and then he names the various regions of the Empire where they lived. James likewise, addresses his words to saints who were away from home but not necessarily by choice (1:1). But in a sense does that not describe us all? Hymnist Albert Brumley reminds us that we are all strangers and pilgrims in a foreign land when he wrote, "This world is not my home, I'm just a passing thru." It's true. We are all forced to live surrounded by circumstances outside of our control and often times beyond our choice. It's the one thing we share in common.

In the light of first-century persecution, Peter and James pen their respective letters to encourage Christians whose circumstances were anything but encouraging. Indeed, in these two letters we find the New Testament counterpart to the Old Testament book of Job. Peter, in fact, mentions "suffering" or words to that effect some fifteen times. Both men seek to put pain into perspective by helping Christians find comfort in the face of personal grief. The details of suffering may differ, but God's abundant grace is constant and is abundantly available to His children—both then and now. "My grace is sufficient for you, for power is perfected in weakness" (2 Cor. 12:9a).

> Consider it joy, my brethren, when you encounter various trials.
>
> —James 1:1

> Blessed be the God and Father of our Lord Jesus Christ, who according to His great mercy has caused us to be born again to a living hope through the resurrection of Jesus Christ from the dead, to obtain an inheritance which is

imperishable and undefiled and will not fade away, reserved
in heaven for you.

—1 Peter 1:3–4

The laughter may stop for a time, but the inner peace and joy lives
on. Our hope lives, writes Peter, because our Jesus lives! It is the one
and only thing that will enable a smile to shine through the pain.

Four Truths About Trials (1 Peter 1:6–7)

1. ***Trials are necessary.*** "*In this you greatly rejoice, even though now for
a little while, if necessary, you have been distressed by various trials*" (1 Pet.
1:6). Sometimes trials are necessary. Sometimes suffering is God's way
of getting our attention that He can get no other way. Sometimes God
uses adversity to forge needed character in His children. Sometimes suffering is His way of teaching us humility and patience and dependence
upon Him. And we need that. "It was good for me to be afflicted, that
I may learn Thy statutes" (Ps. 119:71). Can affliction bring positive
results? Yes. If you let it . . .

James lays down the hard core truth about life when he says,
"Consider it all joy, my brethren, when you encounter various trials."
He doesn't say "if;" he says "when." In other words, if you are experiencing some form of pain, you are the rule, the norm, and the average.
You are certainly not the exception. And God's will being what it is,
there will be more to come. Chances are you don't really want to hear
that but it is the truth. Each of us must pass through the furnace blast
of Heaven's refining fire in order to become what God needs for us to
be. It is not prosperity that forms our character; it is adversity.

Our oldest son knows hardship. From the time he was just a little
guy he has suffered greatly with vision loss—correctable to a certain
level but still a struggle. I remember taking him as a small child to the
specialist at Children's Hospital in Washington, D.C., where he was
first fitted for glasses at age three. As he grew, his vision worsened. As
a young man, he faced the ridicule of peers who went beyond cruel toward a classmate with "Coke-bottle glasses." I'll never forget the day he
was finally able to be fitted for contact lenses. His countenance (which
was positive already in spite of hardship) shone like the sun. And now

as an adult, he has faced the additional surgery of cornea transplants in both eyes. Thanks to the marvels of modern medicine, today he sees better than ever before. But in many ways he was always able to "see" what others missed. In his viewpoint, hardship may knock you down but it is only your attitude that will keep you down. It's not the trials that make or break our lives but how we respond to them. My son has taught me that.

I get a little put out with people who act as if they have cornered the market on suffering. (Ask some people how they are doing and they will tell you—in great detail!) What follows is usually a pitiful sing-song of woe-is-me, "You just don't know . . ." begins the sad refrain and continues with . . . "about the circumstances I'm under." Hmm. May I ask a simple question? If you are a child of hope and heaven, what are you doing *under* your circumstances? As the people of God, aren't we supposed to live *above* our circumstances? Aren't we supposed to smile in the face of adversity and set an example for our mates, our children, our brethren, and our neighbors and friends? I think so. And, lest we forget, aren't we supposed to follow Him who was "the man of sorrows" and who is "acquainted with our grief?"

You are not the only one.

The joy of James and Peter is unconditional and does not depend upon the circumstances surrounding us. This joy rises above. This joy rejoices in spite of suffering because this joy sees beyond this temporary veil of tears. This joy is the only thing that will get you through the grief.

2. *Trials are distressing.* "*You have been distressed by various trials*" (verse 6b). In his excellent work on human suffering, Gerald Sitzer in *A Grace Disguised,* deals with the issue of trivializing another person's trials by comparing pain. He writes, "Though suffering itself is universal, each experience of suffering is unique" (p. 154).

And that is why comparison seldom comforts. The parent who has lost a son to the battlefield of Iraq is not helped to know that your grandfather lost a cousin in WWII. The brother whose home has been flooded and gutted doesn't receive much encouragement from a comparison to the storm of '96 that blew off a few of your shingles.

There are times when silence is golden. There are times to weep tenderly and quietly (Rom. 12:15b). There are times when people need a shoulder more than they need a string of Bible verses. There are times, said the wise man, "to be silent" (Eccl. 3:7b).

The struggles of each of us are personal and real. Very real. We approach with the compassion of Jesus—who never compared trials. "You think you have it rough, your situation is nothing compared to what is facing me in Jerusalem . . ." He never said that. Time and time again He reached across the path of pain to offer a compassionate hand. We must do the same.

3. ***Trials come in various ways.*** ". . . *various trials.*" Our purpose in writing this book is to lean more on the practical than the academic, but let's make one exception. The Greek word for "various" is *poikilos* meaning diverse colors or variegated of diverse sorts (Thayer). We get our word "polka dot" from it. In other and simpler terms, it means that trials will come in a *variety* of shapes and sizes, shades and colors. There is no "one size fits all."

Trials can be physical, emotional, relational, financial, or even spiritual. They may come suddenly like a tornado that drops out of the sky and wipes away a Kansas town, or they may occur over an extended period of time, like a disease that lingers. Trials can be public or they can be private. They can be related to your sin, to someone else's sin, or to no sin at all. Job suffered the loss of his children and his health. King David suffered the loss of his integrity. Hosea suffered the loss of his wife. Early Christians suffered the loss of property. Jesus suffered the loss of His life. But when Paul faced his "thorn in the flesh," God promised him, saying "My grace is sufficient for you" (2 Cor. 12:9a). So He promises us. God has no trouble matching the color of His grace with the particular shade of your trial.

Regardless of what you are facing—God will give you the grace and the strength. And only He can. If you seek solace and comfort any place else, you will not find permanent and lasting relief. It is only by His grace that you will have the strength to arise on the morrow and resume life.

4. ***Trials have a purpose: maturity.*** *"That the proof of your faith, being more precious than gold which is perishable, even though tested by fire, may be found to result in praise and glory and honor at the revelation of Jesus Christ"* (1 Pet. 5:7). It is through the refining fire of God's furnace that our faith is forged. The question is: will we melt away under the pressure of suffering or will we come forth shining as purified gold in the brilliant likeness of the Son? The choice is ours to make.

It is also a choice you have to make and remake each day.

If you think you are going to face your tragedy with renewed faith and grit and that the emotional scars will easily melt away, you are woefully naïve. Like the infamous New Year's resolutions (that last about three days), we deceive ourselves if we think we can solve the problem that quickly. Give yourself a break. Ask the Lord to give you strength for today (He will!). But understand that, come tomorrow, you are going to need more of the same. The faith to keep going is a daily endeavor. But don't quit. As the muscles of your faith get a daily workout, you will eventually feel yourself gaining greater strength. I love Isaiah 40:31—

> Yet those who wait for the Lord
> Will gain new strength;
> They will mount up with wings like eagles,
> They will run and not get tired,
> They will walk and not become weary.

On the wall of my study is a picture of a soaring eagle next to a cliff. And to the side are the words of promise by the prophet Isaiah. What a picture of strength! What a promise of help! "From whence come my help? My help comes from the Lord . . ." But you will need to ask each day. Just remember that if you ask, you will receive!

If we make the right choice of attitude to face our tragedies with the full assurance of faith in the providence of God, then our faith will grow deeper and wiser and, most of all, we will grow up. "God cannot use you greatly until he has broken you completely." I don't know who said it, but it is true. It may be that God is using your tragedy and maturing of your faith so that, in turn, He can use you to help another.

My friend, I do not know what enemies you face this day. But I do know this: if your faith counts for anything, it must count for everything when times are hard. Stand firm in what you know to be true. Ask God to give you the strength for this day. Lay claim to His promise of protection. But do it all with a humble attitude of a servant's heart. "Thy will be done . . ."

Do *you* have that kind of faith? It is the only way to find joy . . . even when the laughter stops.

Chapter 6

In God We Trust
(Sometimes)

WILSON

We talked for a couple of hours. She was a beautiful woman in her mid-fifties who should have been basking in the warmth of life's prime. Her children were raised and doing well, her extended family was strong, her financial situation solid. A strong and dedicated Christian, she lived in a beautiful home surrounded by acres of forest where she lavished her love upon her grandchildren. A fortieth wedding anniversary loomed in her not-too-distant future.

But it all came crashing down.

Marital infidelity is like a huge rock that gets thrown into a tranquil pond—the waves and ripples reach to distant shores. And the waves do not come all at once. It's not "one wave and done." They keep coming. And coming. My friend feels as if she is drowning in a tidal surge of horror. It is unbelievable to her. The pain she faces doesn't go away as the man she trusted and to whom she gave her life and with whom they raised their family—has made the deliberate choice to opt for a much younger woman in search for the elusive fountain of youth that he probably senses is slipping away.

"I just don't understand," she says. And she never will. It is impossible for the logical to comprehend the illogical. "He has turned away from everything he stood for and is making decisions that no one can believe—to the point of questioning spiritual things. He knows

63

better . . ." She is right, he does know better. Knowing, however, isn't the problem. When one declares for a life of sin, knowledge takes a backseat to emotional justification (it's the only way to live with yourself). That is why blame-shifting occurs—"It's really your fault I was driven to this!" and personal comfort becomes primary—"God wants me to be happy!" Rare is the man (or woman) who has the courage to look into the mirror and say with David, "I have sinned" (1 Sam. 12:13; Ps. 51:4).

None of that provides much comfort, however, for the distressed soul left to bob in the wake of more waves that keep coming. "Do you ever want to pull the shades along with the covers and just hide from the world?" I asked. "Yes. *Yes!*" she replied. It's a normal response. Mundane duties that we take for granted—going to the grocery store and making simple choices for meals—become agonizingly painful to the depressed. It's like trying to run when you're up to your neck in water. It is exhausting and you feel as if you are drowning emotionally. And about the time you think you've made progress—another wave, unforeseen and larger than the last, threatens to overwhelm you yet again.

It happens every day and to more people than you can imagine. It may be happening to you or to someone you love.

Don't Forget Your Life Vest

God is real no matter how you feel. Read that again. It is imperative that you engrave that in indelible ink upon your heart because your feelings, acting as a giant eraser, will cause you to question even the most fundamental of truths. Feelings, as valuable and important as they are, can and will betray you. Grab the life vest of this truth and keep it ever near.

It's easy to worship God when everything is great—great family, great friends, great health, and so forth. Praise God! And why not? Life is good and you are happy. It's also easy to worship Him when surrounded by others of like mind. You lift your voice and find it accompanied by a chorus of believers who remind you that you are not alone. Finally, it's easy to worship Him when walking along a quiet beach to the gentle sound of lapping waves or sitting atop a mountain peak and gazing at what seems to be endless vistas. The words to *How Great Thou Art* seem to cascade off the tongue so easily in those mountaintop moments.

I have tough news: those times are rare. In fact, they may be the exception instead of the rule. Want hard truth? My life isn't always great and happy. My voice more times than not has sung alone rather than in a chorus. My beach walks or mountaintop experiences, while I have had them, are sparse when compared to long days and longer nights in the valley. All of which begs the question—*How do you praise God when you don't "feel" like it? How do you maintain a friendship and relationship with Him when He seems so far away, so distant?*

This is where we face the deepest level of worship—finding the ability to praise Him in spite of pain and trials and in spite of our failure to understand the why of life. How do you keep your spiritual focus when your physical world has come crashing down? In other words, how do I love God when I cannot sense His presence and when He feels so far away?

It's not easy.

Absence Makes the Heart Grow . . .

Friendship is tested by separation. That's true in human relationships. A close and dear friend moves away and although you promise each other that you will remain connected and close, time and distance take their toll. Other interests develop. Calls and letters come less frequently. A friendship that once blossomed like flowers in the spring is now reduced to a once-a-year Christmas card greeting—a stark reminder of what used to be and what now is.

True, absence can make the heart grow fonder, but only if it is temporary. Most of the time, it has the opposite effect. And if that is true in *human* relationships, would not the same principle apply in *spiritual* ones?

Here it is: You won't always *feel* close to God. That's hard for Christians to admit but it is true. And when circumstances surround you that leave you reeling with a myriad of emotions—many of which you do not understand—God, it seems, is nowhere to be found. *God, where are You? Why do You leave me when I need you the most?*

That's when worship, praise, and prayer get difficult. And that's when you find out about the depth of your faith and friendship with Him. Here it is: *Can you praise Him when the feelings are not there?*

I am not sure why we struggle with the admission of spiritual loneliness at times. The psalmists certainly acknowledged it. They confessed what we often prefer to hide—that God sometimes seems a million miles away.

> Why dost Thou stand afar off, O Lord?
> Why dost Thou hide Thyself in times of trouble?
>
> —Psalm 10:1

Good questions. At the bottom of this ancient hymn, I long ago scribbled these words of paraphrase: *Why do you hide when I need you the most?* That is exactly what the unnamed psalmist is asking . . . and what we ask in our heart but are too afraid to admit. If there is anything I wish to offer the hurting who experience feelings of abandonment by God, this is it. While those feelings of isolation and abandonment are very real, *your feelings will betray you.* It is a common tool Satan uses when we are most vulnerable. Grab your life-vest: *God is real no matter how you feel*—and hold on to it for dear life. You may be in the water longer than you realize.

> My God, my God, why hast Thou forsaken me?
>
> —Psalm 22:1a

Yes, I know that scholars see this psalm as a foretelling of the fourth of seven pivotal sayings of Jesus from the cross (Matt. 27:46). They are right in its messianic and broader application. But they are only half right. The other half has to do with the man who actually wrote these words—words that poetically describe David's sense of abandonment by God. Read on . . .

> Far from my deliverance are the words of my groaning.
> O my God, I cry by day, but Thou dost not answer;
> And by night, but I have no rest.
>
> —Psalm 22:1b–2

True, there are major differences. Jesus was actually forsaken upon the cross as He bore the burden of sinful man (2 Cor. 5:21; Isa. 59:1–2). Jesus, knowing all things, knew that the Father had turned away, leaving Him to suffer alone. It was not imaginary. David's poetry, on the other hand, lays bare the heart of a man who longs to feel God's nearness but, for whatever reason, does not. I've been there. I bet you have, too.

> For Thou art the God of my strength;
> why hast Thou rejected me?
> —Psalm 43:3

Such thoughts of transparent honesty are sprinkled throughout the poetry section of Scripture. There is no denying them nor is there a deep theological explanation for them—except that God allowed (and encouraged) these men to acknowledge their hearts and journal a record that He would preserve so that the rest of us would understand one simple communicable truth: *we are not the first to have such thoughts.*

You Are Not Alone

The truth in all of this is obvious: God had not abandoned David or the other writers of the hymnal, and God has not abandoned you. The promise of Deuteronomy 31:8 (offered by a man who had twelve decades of first-hand knowledge of God's presence) echoes through the corridors of Old Testament writ: "And the Lord is the One who goes ahead of you; He will be with you. He will not fail you or forsake you. Do not fear, or be dismayed." So strong and imperative is the promise that it is repeated for emphasis sake in the New Testament (Heb. 13:5). God will not leave you. God will not desert you. God will not abandon you. He will not!

That doesn't mean, however, that there will not be times, when you will have *feelings* of isolation, separation, and abandonment. You will. I will. The psalmists did. And while the feelings may seem all too real, they are wrong. Your feelings will betray you.

Have you ever prayed and . . . *nothing?* It can seem so useless; so pointless at times. Have you ever worshipped in an assembly only to leave with a sense of "What's the point" emptiness? Have you ever been so lost in the fog of life's hardships that the shoreline of faith seemed impossible to find—and your cries for help went unanswered? *God, why do You hide when I need You the most?*

I have an amazing revelation for you: *You are normal!* You are as normal as David or the other hymn writers of the psalms. You are as normal as other believers down through the ages who have struggled with the tragedies of life, trying to cope and make sense of the senseless. You are not alone. In fact, it may all be part of God's plan to help us grow in our faith and in our trust of Him. Can you trust God even when you cannot *feel* His nearness?

Time Out

It is imperative at this point that we throw in the disclaimer. Like the ads for product warranties in which the voice-over announcer talks Alvin-chipmunk-like and quickly reels off a paragraph of legalese and fine print, it is essential that we remind ourselves of a single truth that is often plainly and sometimes purposefully overlooked—God may, in fact, be distant from you because of the sinful decisions you have made.

Sin does separate man from God (Isa. 59:1–2). There may be times when you feel disconnected because you, in fact, broke the connection. *You* walked away. *You* distanced yourself. Like the prodigal, *you* left home and traveled to the far country. In other words, don't blame God for something *you* have done.

It's much like the story of the older couple driving along when the wife spots two teenagers snuggling close to one another in the car ahead. "Look at them, Harold," she says in disgust. "Look at them—they have one head!" They ride along further when she blurts out, "Look at us, Harold—look at us! Remember when we used to be like that? And now you're way over there beneath the wheel and I'm way over here next to the door . . ." They ride along a little further when Harold finally clears his throat and calmly announces, "I never moved."

Hmm.

Don't you know there are times when God announces the same to us? The prodigal came home because . . . He had a home to come home to. His Father had never moved. David came back when he tired of lying to himself and everyone else. His Father had never moved. Simon Peter came back because his Father, too, had never moved. You, too, have come back to a Father who has never moved.

It is impossible to comprehend the love of our Father for His children. In spite of our insolence, rebellion, and selfish sinful ways, God stays put. Amazingly, if we wish to walk away, He allows it. More amazingly, if we wish to repent and head for home—He waits with open arms. Like the prodigal boy or the penitent Peter, all of us have, at times, wandered off only to find our way back. And He is there. He hasn't moved.

This, however, is not a discussion of personal sin and its consequences. It is always related, mind you, because sin is always lurking—and you may find yourself on the receiving end of sin's awful consequences, even when you did nothing to deserve it. The innocent victims of drunk driving understand this all too well.

I am discussing feelings of abandonment and estrangement that have nothing to do with sin—at least *your* sin. While not perfect, you haven't done anything to bring on the agony of pain you face. Someone has come along and thrown you overboard and left you to make it on your own. And you are left feeling as if you are all alone, drowning in a stormy sea of billowing waves.

Hear me clearly: *you are not on your own.* Remember faith? Remember the principles of Scripture? Remember how God has been with you all along? That's your life-vest. Grab it. It will always be within reach.

Job

We keep coming back to him, don't we? And for good reason. Like David and the other psalmists, Job, too, writes without façade. There were times when *he* felt disconnected from God.

> Behold, I go forward but He is not there,
> And backward, but I cannot perceive Him;
> When He acts on the left, I cannot behold Him;
> He turns on the right, I cannot see Him.
>
> —Job 23:8–9

Job is asking the same question asked by God's people down through time—*Where is God when I hurt?* Job understood that working through those feelings of disconnect was a vital part of growing his faith. He confessed and didn't hide his feelings (verses 8–9), but also confessed what he knew to be true: "But He knows the way I take; when He has tried me, I shall come forth as gold" (verse 10). Even though Job *felt* like he was alone, he *knew* God was with Him. He did not allow *feelings* to obliterate *facts*.

This passage and others like it highlight a common mistake we all make—we seek a *feeling* more than we seek *Him*. If the feeling is there, we conclude that God is there. But if the feeling isn't there, we conclude that God has abandoned us. Have you ever thought that maybe God chooses to operate outside our feelings at times so we won't always depend upon them? Job did not always *feel* close to God. Ditto for David. Yet even though these great servants did battle with the same emotional struggles faced by you and me, each confessed not only the struggle but also, more importantly, what they knew to be true. Even though God may have *felt* distant, they *knew* He was there. Job continues,

> My foot has held fast to His path;
> I have kept His way and not turned aside.
> I have not departed from the command of His lips;
> I have treasured the words of His mouth
> more than my necessary food.
>
> —Job 23:11–12

Job may not have understood why things happened as they did (he certainly had no inkling of the conversation between Satan and God revealed in chapters one and two) but one thing he knew for sure—he knew that God knew of his plight and he believed that God would ultimately deliver him.

Feelings and Facts

Feelings and facts are two different things. Sometimes there is harmony and we are able to feel what we know to be true. But sometimes feelings are absent and when they are, it is essential that you focus on the facts. Job did. The fact is—God is always present and ever near. His divine presence in our lives is too profound to be measured by the emotional roller coaster of our ups and downs. Truly, God wants you to sense His presence but, more than that, He wants you to *trust* Him even when you can't *feel* Him.

Here it is: There will be situations in life in which your faith will be stretched to the max. There will be times when life knocks you to your knees and you can't take another step. You will question. You will doubt. You will wonder if you will survive today, much less tomorrow. In other words, there will be days when God (if you just went according to your feelings) is nowhere to be found. Your spiritual tank is dry; you're running on fumes.

Job was there. The man lost everything—his family, his livelihood, even his health. For thirty-seven chapters Job tried to figure out the "Why?" and for thirty-seven chapters God said nothing. How do you keep praying and praising Him when life falls apart? How do you keep singing and hoping when you don't understand? How do you find the answers when heaven is silent and you are clueless? Or as one once said, *How do you keep your eyes on Jesus when they are full of tears?*

We must do what Job did.

There are days (and nights!) when you have no choice. You have to walk by the *facts* because the *feelings* are not there.

How? That's really the question, isn't it? *How* do I survive? *How* do I hold my faith together? *How* do I keep my head above water? Better grab the life vest, my friend, and hold on for all it's worth.

Four Things You *Must* Do

1. *Tell God exactly how you feel.* David did—*I feel so alone, so forsaken.* Job did—*I'm angry at God.* Did Job really experience anger toward God?

> Therefore, I will not restrain my mouth;
> I will speak in the anguish of my spirit,
> I will complain in the bitterness of my soul.
>
> —Job 7:11

How do you read that? Those are words of a frustrated man devoid of understanding at life's plight. Job is hurting; Job is angry. Here is a mirror moment: Have *you* ever been hurting and angry—*at God*?

We talk much about the need for friendship with God and yet I fear that most of us know more *about* Him than we really know *Him*. It's akin to the subject of prayer. How easy it is to engage in a comprehensive thirteen-week study of prayer in which we learn everything we need to know to be able to communicate more effectively with God. The only problem is that *knowledge* may not be our problem at all. We know how to pray (that's good); but we don't do it (that's not so good). In the same way, it's easy to know about God but never really know God by developing an up-close and personal relationship with Him. I think churches may be filled with people majoring in the former and neglecting the latter.

How well do you know Him? Do you know Him well enough to trust Him? Do you know Him well enough to reveal your heart to Him?

Have you ever had a friend with whom you could just be yourself? A friend you could trust and reveal your heart to and know that it is okay? A friend you could speak in confidence to about life's deepest hurts and know that your confidence would not be betrayed? God is that friend. In fact, He is such a trusted friend that you can tell Him anything! He can handle everything about you—your doubt, your fear, your anger, your confusion, and your grief. Everything.

He longs for that relationship with you.

Some people must not trust Him. They treat God like a casual acquaintance, and as a result, most prayer conversations with Him are surface. We pray with cliché-ridden words and with vague generalities much like we would talk to an obscure co-worker while waiting at the water cooler. "Nice weather today." "How 'bout them Cowboys!" "Where did you get that suit?" In other words, we exchange courteous pleasantries with God that merely pass the time but not the test. The test is . . . do you know Him well enough to entrust Him with your heart?

I don't know how you parent, but I certainly hope you desire for a better relationship with your children than we sometimes offer our

Father. There are times when I seek communication with my kids and get very little in return. I know and they know something is wrong but they keep it to themselves. Neither do I wish for them to simply repeat the party line and tell Dad what they think I want to hear. Such may sound nice but it is worthless.

I want my children to talk to me. Really *talk* to me. I want to know them, which means I want to know their heart. If they are hurting, I want to know. If they are angry at a decision I have made, I want to know. If they are confused about a situation they deem irresolvable, I want to know. Only when I know and only when they reveal their heart, can we seek a solution and come to a greater understanding.

Sometimes I cannot give them the answers they desire. Sometimes if I explained the basis of my decision they wouldn't understand. Sometimes there are mitigating circumstances involving sensitive information about someone else that they cannot know, and I just have to hold them tight and ask them to do a very hard thing—I ask them to trust me in the absence of understanding. I hope I can be the kind of dad who has earned the right to ask that of them. I know that my heavenly Father has earned the right to ask that of me.

I want my children to understand that they can reveal their heart to me and I will still love them. God did the same for David. And for Job. And He will do that for you. He wants that kind of relationship with you.

Be real with Him. Share your heart. Tell Him exactly how you feel.

2. *Focus on the facts.* Life can get confusing and doubts arise. Like a child who fears the dark and sees a monster behind every tree, we, too, fail to see clearly when our way gets dark and foreboding. There is a symptom among the aged known by health-care professionals as "sundown syndrome." Alzheimer patients or those with other mental health problems often lose an even greater touch with reality when darkness comes. And they aren't the only ones. "Weeping may last for the night, but a shout of joy comes in the morning" (Ps. 30:5). We don't cry ourselves to wake but to sleep.

"Never doubt in the dark what God has told you in the light." Write that down somewhere and remember it. Your fears and feelings will do a number on you in the dark night of the soul. Satan may have a hand in that. Make a deliberate attempt to focus on the facts. There are FACTS about God that you know are true. Always. Without exception.

I know that God is good.
I know that He loves me.
I know that He hears my prayers.
I know that He will not give me more than I can bear.
I know that in the midst of temptation He gives me a way out.
I know that His commandments are not beyond the scope of my obedience.
I know that He is an unmovable, unshakable rock.
I know He cares about me.
I know He has forgiven me.
I know that He is my redeemer and that He lives.

Scattered throughout the book of Job is the patriarch's confession of many of these facts. Consider the last one: "And as for me, I know that my Redeemer lives." A poet by the name of Fred A. Fillmore turned Job's words into a favorite and inspiring hymn. It is a song that is misleading—not in the theme, but in our mental perception of the original author. "I know that my Redeemer lives!"—depicts a mountaintop moment of faith. And indeed it was, but the author was not exactly perched on a mountaintop when he wrote it. When Job penned those words he was in the valley of despair, a hole of darkness wondering if he would ever find his way back to the light. Yet even in the valley of life's hardest days and longest nights, Job focused on the facts and confessed what he knew to be true.

By the way, Job did not write, "I *feel* that my Redeemer lives . . ." He said, "I *know* . . ." He focused on the facts—so must you.

3. *Trust God to keep His promises.* When God says He will do a thing, it's as good as done. Romans 8:28 is one such promise—"And we know (not 'feel') that God causes all things to work together for good to those who love God, to those who are called according to His purpose." Read it on days when you come up empty. Read it on nights when fears beset you. In other words, don't be troubled by trouble!

However bad your circumstances are (and they may be very bad), your situation does not change the character of God or the love of God or anything about God. David and Job both knew that God could be trusted to keep His promises. They also knew that God was for them even when it may not have *felt* like He was.

"*I will never desert you nor forsake you.*" That's a promise that you need to claim. Now.

4. *Remember what He has done for you already.* *If God loved me He wouldn't have . . .* and we add a personal qualification . . . *let my sister die, let my husband leave me, let my body be invaded by cancer . . .* "If?" Let's settle the debate once and for all: if God never did another thing for you, He still deserves your VERY BEST because of what He has already done. And because of what He has already done, He has nothing else to prove.

John 3:16—"*For God so loved the world that He gave His only begotten Son . . .*" The cross. It says everything. Are you worth that? God thinks you are. Whatever you do or however bad it gets, don't question His love. Nothing that ever happens in your life will eclipse His love for you as proven at the cross. He may not be done *with* you but He has already done *for* you. It is a depth of love beyond words.

Some days are harder than others. There are things that have happened in my life that to this day I don't understand—the death of a mother when she was fifty-three-years young; the abandonment of a wife and an unknown future with three children; a prodigal child . . . If trouble comes in a kaleidoscope of colors, I've seen several. I've ridden the emotional roller coaster that some of you are on now and I'm learning a tough lesson—I'm learning the ride isn't over until life is over. We keep saying, "When things level out . . ." Do they ever? Tragedies don't go away. We cover the scars with the clothing of time but they are still there.

And I have had to learn another lesson—that regardless of my feelings, I need to pour them out at His feet. *My Father, I am angry . . . I am confused . . . I am hurt . . . depressed . . . lonely . . .* Keeping them contained within has not helped me. Releasing them into the hands and heart of a Friend in whom I can trust implicitly, has made all the difference.

At those times when I don't know what to do, at least I know where to go—

> Go into your inner room, and when you have shut the door, pray to your Father who is in secret, and your Father who sees in secret will repay you.

There are days when I may not *feel* it but I *know* it—I know He lives and I know He loves me and I know that we'll get through this together. I want you to know that too because I want you to know *Him*.

Don't forget your life vest.

Chapter 7

Good Grief—What's Good About It?

DAVID

We're all familiar with Charles Shultz's comic strip *Peanuts*, and the lament of his lovable character, Charlie Brown, who says, "Good grief!" I don't know whether Charlie Brown coined the phrase himself or just took it from the fabric of our language, but it's an interesting exclamation. Good grief!

Good grief? Isn't that an oxymoron? What in the world can be good about grief? We especially question how it may be good when we're shrouded in the thick fog of heartbreak and sorrow, and the pain of grief is so recent and palpable. How can *anything* good ever come out of grief?

Grief ordinarily focuses on the obvious—loss—and the loss is so bad, we do not generally observe it for anything good. However, with a little effort and the passage of time, you *can* see good come from the most painful of experiences. You may not see it that way right now. You may reason that only bad things can come from your loss, and that no matter what constructive changes result from what has happened, nothing positive can equal what you've lost. I must confess that I felt that way after Adam's death. But I came to realize, and you must eventually understand, that this is not a proposition you may bargain over. The loss has occurred. You cannot change it. You must adjust. You need to heal. If you start to look, you will see positive changes come about because of misfortune and the loss you grieve.

It happened for me. Good came from Adam's death. Good came from Debbie's death. I saw lots of changes for good in me and in others after each of them died. Does that mean I am happy about what happened in our lives? Of course not. But it does mean that God provides for us, even in the most awful of circumstances. As the apostle Paul teaches us, all things work together for the good of those who love the Lord (Rom. 8:28). When I began to see positive changes in me and around me, it helped move my perspective from the center of my boat and the turbulence of my loss to a different plane. It helped me begin to develop a longer and larger view of life's events, which was critical to help me begin healing.

Here are some of the ways my grief worked for good.

Grief Helped Me De-Clutter My Life

Less than a month after we buried Adam, I had a disagreement with my law partner of twenty-plus-years about the division of a substantial sum of money our firm had earned. After we had a long and contentious discussion about it, I told him that under the circumstances I could not remain partners with him, and terminated our business association on the spot. Ordinarily, such an event would have been monumental, a time of great consternation about the day-to-day operation of the business itself, the loyalties of the staff, whether they'd go or stay, the division of files, physical assets, receivables, and other issues attendant to splitting a law firm, not to speak of the impact that termination of our long-term relationship would have on my practice and near-term ability to earn a living.

But it did not affect me that way. All the work issues that might have otherwise kept me awake at night or occupied my mind and caused me to worry meant absolutely nothing to me at the time—not because they were of little value or consequence, but because relatively speaking, they were unimportant. I was grieving the loss of my son. I loved him more than my own life, much less my business. My law practice didn't come close. As I told my partner during that meeting, "This is not the worst thing to happen to me in the last three weeks."

Adam's death made it *easy* for me to recognize the priorities in my life. I didn't have to struggle with the challenges of schedule, or worry about balancing things I *thought* I needed to do with the things I *really* needed to do. Grief made it easy to sort through what was important, less important, and not important at all—to separate the big rocks from the little ones. Adam's death emphasized with an exclamation point, in a way I had never before experienced, that the brevity of life is real and that accountability to God is real. My son's death did not change my priorities in life, but it did sharpen my focus, so that I took more seriously my spiritual life and responsibility. It made me a better person—a better husband, a better father, and a Christian more conscientious about my responsibility to the Lord. Grief drew me closer to God.

King Solomon, the wise author of Ecclesiastes, wrote in Ecclesiastes 7:1–4:

> A good name is better than fine perfume, and the day of death better than the day of birth.

> It is better to go to a house of mourning than to a house of feasting, for death is the destiny of every man; the living should take this to heart.

> Sorrow is better than laughter, because a sad face is good for the heart.

> The heart of the wise is in the house of mourning, but the heart of fools is in the house of pleasure.

Solomon understandably observed that the living should take note that death is the destiny of every man. But still, how can one's death day be better than his birthday, and a place of mourning better than a place of pleasure and joy? Solomon's words seem counterintuitive— exactly the opposite of how we actually feel! Significantly though, his instruction is not designed to teach us how to *feel*; it's designed to teach us how to *think*. In other words, he's helping us develop the proper perspective about life and death, not only about the death of people we love, but, especially, about our own mortality and death. Death, whenever and wherever it happens, reminds us that there is a day of reckoning and accountability, and as Solomon says, it is good to be reminded of that. It is, no doubt, a painful reminder, but that simply helps to underscore how important a matter it is.

That's how it's supposed to work. When we observe death, we face our own mortality. It motivated me to make changes for good in my life, and I saw similar changes in others. Two of Adam's cousins became Christians. Several others in our family and a number of Adam's friends improved their spiritual outlook and made tremendous changes in their lives. Dozens of people shared with us how Adam's life and death impacted them. And those are only the people I know about. Learning the stories of Adam's family and friends helped us to visualize the ripple effect our son had left, and helped begin to relieve the awful sting of his loss. Of course, there was a lot of healing left to be done, but the changes for good in our lives and the lives of others was an important step in our healing process.

Grief Helped Me Capture "Today"

When I was growing up, my father did not frequently say that he loved me or my brothers, although I never questioned whether or not he did. The few times he said it—less than a handful—were awkward, albeit sincere. In the same way, after my sons were born, I did not tell them I loved them as frequently as I should have, particularly after they reached adolescence, although I know they knew it. It just did not seem to be the thing that men do. However, that changed immediately when Adam died.

I specifically recall that the last thing I said to Adam the fateful evening he left for IU was, "Be careful—and don't get a ticket." I should have said, "I love you." After his accident, I repeatedly told Kyle and Colin that I loved them because I wanted to reinforce it and be sure they knew it. I still tell them that to this day. It cannot wait to a later time; it needs to be said today. At the end of every text message and e-mail I write, "Love, Dad." At the end of every telephone call I say, "I love you, son." Before we part company I say, "I love you, son." I'm confident that my sons would know that I love them even if I didn't say it to them, but I need not leave it to guesswork. I want them to remember not just that I loved them, but what it was like to *hear* me say it, and I want them to model that behavior for their children.

Today, I can't tell Adam that I love him, but I can say it to my other sons and others dear to me in life. I must learn from that and take advantage of today. "This is the day the Lord has made; let us rejoice and be glad in it" (Ps. 118:24).

Grief Helped Me Value My Family More

How many times have you observed death shatter a family? We've all seen it happen: a child dies; the parents eventually divorce; siblings lose focus and wander aimlessly through life. It doesn't happen every time, nor does it happen just like that, but we've all seen it happen. I don't pretend to understand the science of it all, nor will I attempt to explain the whys. I just know it can happen. Experience has taught me that grief makes it very easy to retreat into your own self-absorbed world, where you shut yourself off from those around you, even those you love, and simply drift away. It's easy to focus on *my* loss, *my* hurt, *my* pain, so much so that when you do interact, your behavior is very *me*-centered. Eventually, relationships can stand only so much of that kind of selfishness and they begin to fall apart. When you're thrust into such a position, you must guard against it.

Fortunately for me, Adam's death helped me take stock to realize just how much I loved my family, the people closest to me in life. It helped me to better translate their value into action, and to hone an others-centered mindset. In other words, it improved the way I behaved toward them. Loss helps you recognize pettiness for what it is. Valuable relationships are not worth hurt feelings over small or insignificant matters—and in the great scheme of things, there is little that is not small or insignificant. Consequently, before I reflexively reacted to some event or remark, I tried to make an even greater effort to measure myself and ask, "Is this disagreement more important to me than his or her feelings? Is this issue more valuable to me than our relationship?" Of course, the answer was almost always "no."

That perspective helped me as a husband and father to do my part to reduce and avoid the potential for unrest in our family, especially at a time when we needed calm. Instead of selfishness and discord pushing us apart, selflessness and peace helped to pull us together. We needed to be knit in a tightly woven fabric of reliance and dependence on each other to survive the crushing, destructive forces death can have on a family unit. In fact, we specifically discussed that as a family Adam's death would either draw us closer or it would shatter us—one or the other. We determined we would not let it destroy us. We survived not because of my single-handed effort to hold us together, but because, with God's help, each one of us understood what was at stake.

Grief presents a unique growth challenge. Can you control your personal pity party? Can you focus on your family's needs? It is an extraordinary occasion to grow or shrink, to mature or fail. Even in the midst of the pain of sorrow, I found an opportunity for good with the relationships in my family. Clearly, they were worth the effort.

Grief Helped Me Pray More

Following Adam's accident, I prayed all the time. I understood for the first time in my life what Paul really meant when he wrote *"pray without ceasing"* (1 Thess. 5:17). I prayed at bedtime; I prayed getting up; I prayed when I lay awake in the middle of the night. I prayed in the shower and before I ate meals; I prayed while driving and while sitting at work. I hurt so badly and needed relief so much that I had to talk to God about it. I didn't know what else to do.

I found encouragement in passages like Psalm 62:5–8, in which David described the trustworthy pathway to security and hope:

> Find rest, O my soul, in God alone; my hope comes from Him. He alone is my rock and my salvation; He is my fortress, I will not be shaken. My salvation and my honor depend on God; He is my mighty rock, my refuge. Trust in Him at all times, O people; pour out your hearts to Him, for God is our refuge.

I prayed for God to lift the unbearable weight of grief and sorrow from me and asked Him to heal my heart. And I prayed it over and over. I read and relied on Psalm 55:22: "Cast your cares on the Lord and He will sustain you; He will never let the righteous fall." I remembered that James 4:8 says that if we draw near to God, He will draw near to us. God is not unfamiliar with our suffering, and He will care for and comfort us. God, even God, knows what it is for His Son to die.

Grief caused me to pray more and depend on God more. It drew me closer to Him, and that was a change for good.

Grief Helped Me Help Others

When Paul wrote 2 Corinthians 1:3–4, he penned a beautifully instructive passage to help the grieving find genuine comfort:

> Praise be to the God and Father of our Lord Jesus Christ, the Father of compassion and the God of all comfort, who comforts us in all our troubles, so that we can comfort those in any trouble with the comfort we ourselves have received from God.

You want to heal and find hope in the middle of tragedy and sorrow? Help someone else find it! You want to climb out of the deep hole of pain and depression you're in? Help lift someone else out of theirs. It is the Lord's recipe for healing.

God has equipped each of us to serve a purpose He wants us to serve. A collection of scripture teaches the principle, but 2 Timothy 2:21 and 3:17 suffice. A couple of examples show the principle in the lives of real people. In Jeremiah 1:4–5, Jeremiah records that the Lord had a special purpose for him—a purpose Jeremiah fulfilled: "The word of the LORD came to me saying, 'Before I formed you in the womb I knew you, before you were born I set you apart; I appointed you as a prophet to the nations.'" David knew, even when pursued by King Saul, that God intended for him to serve a special purpose (Ps. 57:3; 138:8), and David served the purpose God wanted him to serve. Acts 13 records a speech Paul made at the synagogue at Pisidia Antioch, and in verse 36, Paul said, "For when David had served God's purpose in his own generation, he fell asleep; he was buried with his fathers and his body decayed." Paul's discourse was designed to lead his audience to faith in Jesus and His resurrection, and that's why he mentioned David's death, but we should not ignore what he said about David's life: "*When David had served God's purpose . . .*"

The story is the same for others in the Bible: Pharaoh (Rom. 9:17); Paul (Acts 26:16–20; 1 Tim. 2:7; 2 Tim. 3:10); Jesus (John 17:4). And there are more. We shouldn't be surprised. Scripture teaches that God knows every detail about us (Ps. 139:13–16), even when and where we'll live (Acts 17:26–27), all so that we might, perhaps, seek after Him and find Him. Some, like David, served their special purpose; others, like the Pharisees and legal experts of Luke 7, did not (Luke 7:29–30). Whatever the case, God's purpose will still be accomplished; somebody will fulfill the special purpose He intends (Isa. 46:11), because His purposes will not fail (Prov. 19:21).

Moreover, the roles and purposes God has designed for us come in all shapes and sizes: service to others, teaching, encouraging, generosity, leadership, mercy, rejoicing, mourning (Rom. 12:4–8,15), to name just a few. The list goes on and on.

Why is all of that important? Because, of course, it eventually leads to *me*. Did God designate a purpose just for people in the Bible? Did God not know *me* before I was born? Did He not know *you*? The answers, really, are obvious.

What job or role has He purposed for me? To answer that question, I ask myself this: What has He equipped me to do? I may not be able to speak with 100 percent certainty when I give an answer, but I know that I have a greater capacity to help someone who suffers with grief and loss than someone who hasn't experienced it. I know that I can speak to the heart of one who hurts just like I have. I know because I've done it. And I can connect to the hurting heart not because I have some special ability, but because I've walked a mile in the shoes of those who hurt.

I think of my friend Ferrell, whose twenty-year-old son died in a tragic accident. When I saw him afterward, he hugged me so tightly and whispered through his tears that he had thought of me. "I know you've been here. It hurts so bad," he said. Or my friend Freddie, whose courageous daughter discovered during her pregnancy that she had cancer, but refused treatment for the safety of her unborn child and then died giving birth. "What a small, awful fraternity we have," Freddie said as we embraced. Or Randy, whose twenty-something children both died in the same night in separate auto accidents. As he sat at the funeral home in a state of absolute shock, surrounded by loving friends, I touched his shoulder and met his gaze with an understanding nod. "There's a man," he said, "who knows how I feel."

What have I done that's so special? Nothing. I just happened to walk in the shoes that they now wear. I know how they fit and how they hurt. I can help them bear the load. And every time I leave the side of someone whose heart is bursting with sorrow, I feel better for having been there, thankful that the awful wounds I've experienced have helped me carry someone else's burdens, even if for a short distance. Since I'm equipped to serve others that way, I try to see that as at least a part of the purpose I can serve for God. That's what you can do now, too.

You may not feel ready to do it yet. That's okay, but don't wait too long. You may have to push yourself to get up and go. That's alright, but be sure you do it. You may not know what to do or how to do it. Don't worry. You'll figure it out when you get there.

I'm no expert, but I have a few suggestions, even for those who haven't experienced heart-wrenching loss.

Just go. So many times people avoid the uncomfortable environment of death and loss. What do you say to someone whose child just died? "I'm so sorry," works; "I hurt so much for you." Truthfully, however, you don't have to say a word. You just need to be there. Hold them. If you've walked a mile in their shoes, say, "I know," because you do. Tell them it hurts, but it will get better. You know, because it does. You don't have to spell out a time schedule. There isn't one. You don't have to have magic words of encouragement. There aren't any. They just need you to be there.

When Adam died, over a thousand people came to our home and poured through the funeral chapel to comfort us. We were overwhelmed with their concern and love. One of Adam's high school friends came through the receiving line at the funeral home to express his sympathy. "I know how you feel," he said. "My uncle died three months ago." Well, I knew he didn't really know how I felt, but I knew he wanted me to know that he hurt for us, and he sympathized with us in the best (and only) way he could connect with our feelings. I was thankful for his thoughtfulness. Friends from hundreds of miles away drove to be with us and share in our heartbreak. Hundreds from our community and across the country, some of whom we didn't even know, wrote notes of condolences. Day after day for several weeks, our mailbox was literally full. Every card lit a small candle of hope in our hearts. I learned firsthand what "mourn with those who mourn" really means, and what an encouragement it can be.

My friend Bill Robinson, an evangelist who now lives in Birmingham, called me the morning after Adam's accident, when the shocking news was racing through our network of friends. He was in San Francisco, gazing from the island of Alcatraz at the beautiful skyline of the city. He offered in tears to come immediately to our side. It was Bill who first shared with me the perspective that became so important to healing. He told me, "I cannot understand why things happen the way they do. I sort of view the events of time as a great tapestry, and our lives as threads in its picture. The whole tapestry is too large for us to comprehend, but our individual threads are still important to make the picture what it is. I don't know how, but somehow, this thread makes a difference." He described a truly complicated concept in a very simple way, and encouraged me more than he could ever know while we suffered through the deepest part of our sorrow. Thankfully, he—and hundreds of others—weren't afraid to dive in and share our tears.

Despite the gracious willingness of friends and Christians to share our horrible grief, however, the people I sought out were my friends who'd lost children. They could tell me—with authority—that the horror would diminish and that joy would eventually return to our lives. It was a message we needed desperately to hear over and over, and it helped sustain us. Those friends were right, but because we couldn't see much past our immediate pain at the time, we took them at their word and leaned on God to carry us. The unique understanding and encouragement we received from each one was so valuable. That is the unique position I'm now in to help those who hurt with the same kind of loss, and the position you now share with me.

Be kind. Our church family, friends, and co-workers showered us with food and acts of kindness. One young man promised to mow our yard for a year—and he did. Another cut us several ricks of firewood to get us through the winter. Several lady friends came to our home and, without asking or saying a word, undertook Debbie's normal housekeeping tasks because they knew she couldn't do it—not then. Those simple acts of kindness and expressions of love meant so very much at a time when we were desperately low.

Ironically—and not surprisingly—those same people rushed to our side five years later when Debbie fell into a coma and died. Scores of people—family and friends—sat in vigil at the hospital, some all through the night, to encourage us and pray for us. Once again, we were inundated with the humbling kind of love, care, and concern that leaves you feeling speechless and so undeserving.

Ask to see a picture. One of the most uncomfortable social moments we may encounter is when we meet someone for the first time, and after asking about their children, they awkwardly tell us that they lost a son or daughter. That always seems to be a conversation stopper. One of the things I now do, and encourage others to do, is ask to see their child's photo and to tell me about him or her. Like most parents, I like to talk about my children, and the opportunities to do that diminish when your child has died. If I happen to be at the mall or the grocery and see someone I haven't seen for a while, it's not unusual for them to ask how Kyle and Colin are doing. Obviously, though, no one asks how Adam is doing.

When I've asked to see a photo, almost without exception I receive expressions of relief and thanksgiving for the chance to open up and freely speak about their dear one, an opportunity that doesn't come very often. Some may still bear a great deal of pain so that it's hard to discuss their loss. That's the way it was for Debbie, even after Adam had been gone for several years. If that's the case, they'll politely tell you. But they'll be thankful that you thought enough to ask them to share, even if they shed a tear or two. Do not let your fear of touching a difficult subject keep you from reaching out. After all, you've been there and walked a mile in their shoes.

Finally, be sure you keep a photo of your loved one handy. Every time you ask to see a picture is an opportunity to share your own. You will connect with your friend in ways you never imagined, and while you help them bear their burdens, you'll heal yourself as well.

What has God purposed for you? What has He equipped you to do? You have to answer those questions for yourself, but I can tell you with certainty that you'll never heal faster than when you help someone else to heal.

Praise be to the God and Father of our Lord Jesus Christ, the Father of compassion and the God of all comfort, who comforts us in all our troubles, so that we can comfort those in any trouble with the comfort we ourselves have received from God.

—2 Corinthians 1:3–4

What beautiful words of encouragement. I hope you put them into practice.

The Conclusion of the Matter Is This . . .

There are many other changes—good things—that flowed from the tragedies we experienced, some of which I'll discuss later. For now, though, I trust you have insight into the meaningful ways that good can result from bad. Have you noticed changes for good in yourself or those near you that resulted largely from your loss? Believe it or not, good—somewhere, somehow—will come from your loss. If you look around hard enough, you'll see it. You may not see it immediately, but it will come. That doesn't mean there's no hardship or sadness, or that you should try to create some sense of happiness about tragedy in your life. But it does mean that there's room for thankfulness about small blessings, even in the pit of grief, and that God can use some of the greatest misfortunes in life in ways we cannot imagine. You must trust Him. Will you allow your grief to make you a better person, improve your relationships and your devotion and service to God? You decide. I hope you will.

Chapter 8

The Process— Getting Stuck in an Emotional Time Warp

WILSON

Get over it!" "Snap out of it!" "Time heals all wounds." "If it were me, I would . . ." Who hasn't been on the receiving end of those who are often all-too-quick to offer over-the-counter advice? Grief is a very complicated and misunderstood emotion, often taking years to traverse. Those who think it can be reduced to a neat list of absolute definitions, timelines, strategies, and completion dates have obviously never tried to survive the rolling waves of emotional pain. Like the arrogance of Eliphaz, Bildad, and Zophar (Job's three friends who thought they had all the answers when, in reality, they failed to grasp the questions), so it is with our friends who sometimes offer counsel when perhaps silence would better be suited.

We call Helen each Sunday night. While it has been a year since an accident claimed Ron's life, the shocking news of that morning remains fresh in our memory, re-playing itself each day. "How do I go on?" our friend asks. "The girls alternate between crying and anger—even anger at their dad for taking his motorcycle on such a cold and icy morning." Then she adds, "And while we appreciate the kindness of everyone, it seems almost unfair to watch the lives of others return to normal while we are stuck—held captive to the tragedy of that day."

Crying. Anger. Unfair. Stuck. Held captive. Like so many others, she is making her way through the maze of grief. And it is a very slow and agonizing process. And sometimes you do get stuck.

Grief Stages

Elizabeth Kubler-Ross (who pioneered the hospice program of care for the dying) is famous for identifying five stages of grief experienced when a patient is given a terminal prognosis.

- **Denial** (this isn't *happening* to me!)
- **Anger** (why is this happening to *me?*)
- **Bargaining** (I promise to be a better person *if . . .*)
- **Depression** (I don't *care* anymore.)
- **Acceptance** (*I'm ready* for whatever comes.)

While it is true that we may experience some or all of these emotions as we face various trials, it is also true that there is no script for grief. (Would that it were that easy.) Grief is as individual as the human fingerprint. There is no one-size-fits-all. The grieving process of a family losing a ninety-year-old grandfather who suffered long with Alzheimer's is quite different from that of a wife whose husband is suddenly and tragically killed in an accident on his way to work. Then again, her grief will differ from that of a parent who loses a marriage and tries to survive a divorce while raising children alone. Grief is as individual as those who feel it and as varied as the circumstances and situations that surround it.

There are, however, some common denominators.

And there is always a process.

When Will I Get Over This?

It is a common question with a complex answer. The truth is, you're not going to wake up one morning to find that all the hurt, pain, and nasty has disappeared. We never forget the person for whom we grieve. Never. Our feelings may be tempered by time as more good memories than sad flood our daily thoughts but . . . who isn't to say that there won't also be times when we have taken two steps forward only to fall back three A song, a picture, a friend from days past—and suddenly moments of raw emotion whisk you back to a previous "stage" you thought had been left behind. Normal? Yes.

There is no completion date to the grieving process. Read that again. We don't like that because we want it to be neater and more definitive. And we try to make it that way with unwritten societal rules (although unwritten they are very much enforced), such as 1) a widower cannot date and certainly not marry for one full year; 2) widows must wear dark and drab clothing as a sign of mourning; and 3) laughter and fun times are the surest sign of disrespect for the departed. The truth is that such rules are man-made and may actually hinder the grieving process.

It is also important to note that men and women handle grief differently. Men tend to keep it all inside while women tend to be more expressive with others. That is why, on average, when a man loses a spouse to death versus when a woman loses the same, widowers will generally remarry sooner. And are usually criticized for it.

It all goes back to our genetic differences. A man by nature, and because he tends to keep things within, confides and shares his life and heart with only one person—his spouse. She is his soul mate. Women, on the other hand, are more emotionally open and frequently share their feelings with other women friends. Women gather at pretty-as-pink tea rooms and openly cry about their loss and hardship. And what does a man do? He meets a buddy for lunch at the corner Mexican restaurant and over three bowls of chips and a burrito shares his innermost feelings about NASCAR, hunting, fishing, football, and politics. A woman goes home alone but feels renewed. A man goes home alone and feels sick to his stomach—*it must have been the burrito!*

It was God who said: "It is not good for man to be alone." The Creator understood what we fail to comprehend—a man shares his heart with only one. And when she dies, something within him dies, too.

Ironically, when a man remarries, it is a testimony to a life lost that he seeks to regain. Rather than being an act of disrespect for the dead, it is in fact a high compliment to the previous relationship. He wants desperately to find his heart and live again. He may not be able to verbalize it, but he knows it.

Contrary to what some think, it is not usually about sexual attraction. Most of the time it is about companionship—someone to talk and share with. Sure, some make foolish choices and do so too quickly. And it is never a good thing to make such life decisions while progressing through the denial or anger stages of grief. There comes a time, however, when that decision can be made with a clarity of mind and it is usually in the best health-interest of both parties.

Aude McKee, my good friend, married again in his late seventies. (The last time he dated was during the Hoover administration!) My wife knew something was up when he bought a new Buick with, in his own words, "one of those new-fangled miniature record players" (CD player). "You just bought yourself a date-mobile," she joked. He smiled. And kept smiling because his life had returned. He was able to move on. In a strange sort of way, it probably saved his life—or at least extended it several more years.

The same was true for my dad. And for David. And me. Circumstances are always different, but the male need for companionship is always the same.

That is why families must work hard to be more understanding and less critical of those who struggle. "If it were me . . ." The truth is, it is *not* you, and you have no idea how you would respond in similar circumstances. Grief is a very private and individual journey. And because it has forever changed your life, you will always be a work in progress.

Help! I'm Stuck . . .

One of the problems we have encountered while interviewing and talking with various people in preparation for this project is the number of people who have become (for lack of a better word) "stuck" in one of the grief stages. And it happens in any kind of grief—whether death, divorce, or disease. With some, life grinds to a halt and never does begin again. Every conversation they have and everything they do relates to the accident, the disease, the trauma, and tragedy. It's like they live in a perpetual time warp. They are stuck.

"The tragedy" becomes their reference point and defines who they are. Regardless of conversation, it always returns eventually to "the tragedy." Close ties and friendships that were once strong are sometimes less so because of the inability of the hurting one to move on. At first, and for some time, we make allowances for the grieving and grant to them the privilege of time and space. But eventually it becomes obvious that they are "stuck" while the rest of the world has moved ahead. To the hurting it seems that people are unfair and uncaring. The truth is—others recognize a very hard truth: life moves on. For the health and well being of everyone, it must move on.

Denial

Denial doesn't usually last that long, as the ongoing process of life, like winds billowing the sails of a ship, has a way of moving us along. Because we have to eat and make a living, the shock wears off and we are forced to accept reality and face forward. There are exceptions and those who become locked in this stage need experienced and professional help.

Those prolonging denial usually turn their rooms/homes into a museum of memories. Out of respect for the dead, they reason, it is important that everything remain just as it was. But it isn't healthy.

After my mother died from cancer at the young age of fifty-three, my father handled her death as well as anyone ever could. In that regard, he set an example for his sons that we will always remember. Years later he would write a brief book: *Troubled Over Many Things—(Connie W. Adams, Guardian of Truth publications)* that has helped scores of people. In it he addresses the problem of those who are stuck in denial—

> Beware of the shrine. Some try to cope by sealing off a room, leaving everything as it was and resisting any effort by family members to change a thing. Over the long haul this is not healthy. If there are other family members still at home, this is not fair to them. When my first wife died, one of the hardest things of all was to clear out her closet. I folded every item myself, placed it in boxes and, by mutual agreement, gave them to my sister-in-law. Every piece stirred a memory. We had a guest room in which she had made the curtains and the

bedspread and arranged the furnishings. But it continued to be used as a guest room. At first I would stand in the room and look at what she had made and relive memories. But they were not made for a museum. They were made to use. I have known of widows who sealed off a workshop and would not allow anything to be touched. This will prolong your agony and hinder the acceptance of reality.

He is 100 percent right. While denial is the birthplace of the grief process, we must not allow it to become our final resting place. As odd as it may seem, respect for the one we have given up is best seen when we give ourselves permission to move forward. There will be plenty of memories to cherish, but it is essential that we also make new ones.

Anger

Anger is a different breed. In the event of divorce, we may want to fight back or get even with our former spouse and thus revenge becomes an all-consuming passion. In the event of a death, we may become angry with the deceased—blaming them for leaving us in this mess. Or we may become angry at the fact that we were spared in the accident while another died. Or we are angry at God—"If God really loved me, He wouldn't have let the accident happen . . ." Anger is a natural part of the grieving process and should not be short-circuited. "Be angry, and yet do not sin . . . and do not give the devil an opportunity" (Eph. 4:26–27). The greatest door of opportunity we can ever give the deceiver of mankind is when we harbor anger and refuse to let it go.

I spoke at a Texas gravesite for a young couple that only days before had rejoiced at the birth of their baby girl. It was short-lived as the little girl developed serious health problems and passed away. I remember her precious look of innocence as she lay in a miniature white casket while wearing a matching white lace dress. In one way it was an easy funeral to conduct, for none of us had any doubt that she was safe in the arms of God. In another way, however, it was an odd service—in that children are supposed to live, not die. That's why I chose to do something different. Instead of the more formal "preacher behind the podium" stance of orthodoxy, I walked to where they were seated, knelt beside them and just talked, read Scripture, and prayed. It was a brief and needed moment of private intimacy.

I will never forget something else.

After the concluding comments at the gravesite, the parents stood around that little casket, said their goodbyes, and then released a large balloon into the bright blue Texas sky. They watched until it finally disappeared from view. We all did. No one moved. Or spoke. It was a poignant moment that symbolized letting go and moving on.

I am not so shallow as to believe that each of us can solve our problems of anger by merely releasing a balloon and watching it float away. But the truth is—each of us does have a choice as to how long we will hold onto our anger and a choice as to when we will let it go. And you can let it go. You may need to get down upon your knees (literally!) and confess your anger at God. By the way, He already knows you are mad at Him. Tell Him. Pour forth both heart and tears and lay them at His feet. There is nothing He cannot handle. But remember: God cannot help you heal until you first become honest with Him.

Are you angry with a former spouse who abused you or who never loved you? Take those feelings, likewise, to the throne. Confess your heart. Lay it bare before God. Some have found help in symbolically discarding a memento from days gone by. If that helps you, do it. Some have accelerated the healing process by making changes—new bedroom furniture, travel, a project of interest, reaching to others, etc. Changes can and should be made, but only when you are ready. You cannot short-circuit the process. You will know. And God will help you know. "If any lack wisdom, let him ask of God" (James 1:5).

Depression

Many of those dealing with tragic loss fall into the pit of depression—a place of overwhelming hopelessness and resignation. The psalmist spoke poetically about the lowland of depression when he admitted what we often try to hide: "My soul cleaves to the dust" (Ps. 119:25). That is depression. Some of God's greatest servants battled this debilitating emotion—Moses, Jeremiah, David, Elijah, Jonah, and others. The sons of Korah wrote, "O Lord, the God of my salvation, I have cried out by day and in the night before Thee . . . For my soul has had enough troubles . . . I have become like a man without strength, forsaken among the dead . . . Thou hast put me in the lowest pit, in dark places, in the depths" (Ps. 88:1–6).

If the "greats" of the Bible had their down time and blue Mondays; days when they couldn't get up out of the pit, why does it surprise us that we have the same trouble? Depression is sticky and it's easy to get stuck.

For example, self-pity surfaces as you see others enjoying good health and good times and you wish desperately for the same. The simple scene of a couple holding hands in the store may trigger a pity party as you realize now more than ever that we live in a "couple" world, and you sense that you're on the outside looking in.

Depression, however, is natural. Like an e-mail that arrives with an attachment, depression is acceptance with an *emotional* attachment. You can't avoid it or delete it. It must be opened. It must be faced.

Depression doesn't arrive with a quick and easy fix. You don't arise in the morning, greet the new day with a Scriptural quotation—"This is the day the Lord has made, let us rejoice and be glad!"—and *presto!* Goodbye depression, hello hope. It doesn't work that way.

A few need medical help to conquer it. Sometimes Christians view physicians that treat the mind as spiritually suspect (although we're hesitant to admit it). "Just read your Bible and pray!" is the quick-and-easy answer given as the cure-all to every problem. The bottom line . . . prayer *is* the cure-all to every problem, *but*—there are some experiencing the depth of depression to such a point that a chemical imbalance has occurred requiring medical attention. And that's okay. God has provided mankind with wonderful discoveries of science that have helped to lift the grieving out of the valley and back to level land. We praise Him for what He has allowed us to discover and learn.

Most, however, find themselves seated next to Elijah of old— knocked to the knees with debilitating circumstances that would depress anyone. If we could see, however, the factors that led to Elijah's depression and what he did about it, it might help us. The scene is found in 1 Kings 19 . . .

How Did It Happen?

1. *He stopped thinking clearly.* Threatened by the wicked queen Jezebel, the prophet ran for his life. He was alone, scared, weary, and exhausted. Slumping beneath a juniper tree he begged God to take his life—"It is enough now, O Lord, take my life . . ." (verse 4b). Rather than considering the source in light of the power of God, Elijah crawled into the cave of depression. Verse 3 tells us why—"And he was afraid . . ." Fear is debilitating—fear of the unknown . . . fear of "Where do I go from here?" . . . fear of "What if . . .?" Ironically, there is nothing in this scene about prayer. Elijah forsook the secret weapon held by every child of God—the power of prayer. "Is anyone among you suffering? Let him pray" (James 5:13a). Prayer is like the sun, in that it clears away the fog. It keeps the fog of depression from settling.

2. *He separated himself from his friends,* verses 3-4a. Why is it that when we get discouraged, we tend to isolate ourselves? There are two facts you must consider: 1) depression feeds on loneliness, and 2) we gain strength from relationships. It is essential that when passing through the fire of grief you stay connected with family and friends. "Two are better than one . . . for if either of them falls, the one will lift up his companion" (Eccl. 4:9–10). It may mean that you have to take the initiative. Take it. Pick up the phone and call. Meet for lunch. Send the e-mail. Get involved more than ever with the church or a Bible study group. Stay connected to people.

3. *He fell into the trap of self-pity.* Elijah was stuck. "I am not better than my fathers" (verse 4b). By the way, whoever said he had to be, or made up that rule? "And I alone am left." He said that twice! (verses 10,14). Elijah felt as though he was the only one facing his crisis.

I've known a lot of Elijahs! Like the prophet, they have decided that they are the only ones to ever face such a tragedy—chemotherapy, a prodigal child, Alzheimer's, a debilitating accident, more surgery. "I am the only one . . ." I mean no disrespect to the suffering when I say— Nonsense! You are not the only one. True, your suffering is unique because you are unique, but you are not the first to so suffer. Why is it that some people face the most awful of tragedies and survive with a smile and others develop the "Eeyore" disposition of that notable donkey in Winnie the Pooh? Circumstances you cannot choose; attitude toward those circumstances *is* your choice. In Elijah-like fashion, however, we complain that we are the only one.

I am convinced that some do that long after the fact because they sense it gives them attention. And it does—but not the positive kind they want. Soon they find the attention span of friends has lessened, as patience wears thin. There comes a time to move on.

"I have every right to be depressed" is the sentiment echoing throughout the chapter. God listened and was patient with His servant. And then He did something to help His man move along.

What Did God Do?

1. *God prescribed rest and food,* verses 5–6. It's amazing how much better we feel when we take care of our physical self. You can let yourself freefall into the pit, or you can grab on to the ledge and start the slow and agonizing climb back to the top. Survivors are not those who give up or in. Neither are they super men and women. Survivors are those who believe that life, regardless of the hardships and tragedies, is worth the living. And so they climb. Sometimes the mountain is daunting and the way is steep and the only climbing that can be done is on one's hands and knees. It can be painfully slow. Sometimes the path skyward is muddy and slick and the lack of a foothold sends one sliding backward and the climber must begin again. It's never easy to climb a mountain. It was Sir Edmond Hillary who, after a failed attempt at Mt. Everest, addressed the giant that towered above him: "I am going to do this because . . . you are as big as you will ever get—and I'm still growing!" He climbed and conquered. You can, too!

2. *God communicated gently,* verses 11–13. It is interesting that God spoke to Elijah with gentleness and compassion. He could have roared in the wind—"but the Lord was not in the wind." He could have impressed the prophet by showing His presence in the earthquake—"but the Lord was not in the earthquake." He could have shown His power in the

scorching heat of fire—"but the Lord was not in the fire." Where was He? Are you ready for this?

> And after the fire a sound of a gentle blowing . . . and it came about when Elijah heard it, that he wrapped his face in his mantle, and went out and stood in the entrance of the cave. And behold, a voice came to him and said, "What are you doing here, Elijah?"
>
> —verses 12b–13

There was no: "Get up and get on your feet, you bumbling prophet! Snap out of it and quit your bellyaching!" God knew Elijah needed calm reassurance. He knows you need it, too.

3. *God made Elijah feel needed again,* verses 15–16. "Elijah, you're still valuable to Me. You're still in my plans. There's work I need for you to do. And, by the way, you're not the only one trying to do right" (verse 18). "There are 7,000 people who need you and if they do not hear My Word from you, then from whom?" Depression has a way of leaving one with a sense of debilitating uselessness. God helped His prophet to see what the fog had obscured. There was still a reason to live. There were still people who loved and needed him. And there were still reasons to get up each morning.

I don't know what turmoil and tragedy you face today, but I'll tell you this—God will give *you* a reason to get up and "Go . . ." just like He did for Elijah. And unless I miss my guess, while there may not be 7,000 people depending upon you, I bet there are several who would like nothing better than to see you busy, active, and alive again. It will be the best gift you could give them.

4. *God gave Elijah a new friend,* verse 19. "*So he departed from there and found Elisha . . .*" You have no way of knowing what God has planned for you. Elijah thought his life was useless and over. Not so. If he could climb from the pit of depression, so can you. After all, we serve a God with unlimited power. A God so strong and powerful that He can "redeem your life from the pit" (Ps. 103:4).

I think of David, my co-author and friend, that at this moment writes across the hall. Today is one of the few we had scheduled as a joint writing day to put the finishing touches on this book. As you know by now, he is no stranger to grief. Neither was his wife-to-be, a beautiful Alabama lady living in obscurity (at least to David) who had already come to terms with living the rest of her days as a single mom and grandmother. We believe it was more than mere fate or chance that brought them together to heal. We believe it was God's providence.

Ditto for me.

Like Elijah, there was a time when I believed that life as I knew it was over. My effectiveness for God could never be reclaimed. But He knew better. As I accepted my life for what it was, I came to see His power greater than ever before. As mentioned previously, "God cannot use you greatly until He has broken you completely." He broke the Twelve who had been squabbling over supremacy in the Kingdom, humbled them, reshaped them, and made them stronger than ever before. God is still in the humbling and reshaping business. He changes lives in ways we never thought possible.

Are you stuck? The sooner you accept the reality of your life as it is today and embrace the hand of the living God, the sooner you will find your way back. That doesn't mean that life will ever be the same or that things will "return to normal." It won't and they won't. It does mean that you will adapt and trust Him to lead you to higher ground.

Five Things You Must Do to Dig Out:

1. ***Remind yourself "I am not the only one."*** Not only do the stories of Scripture refresh our memory with that important thought, but also the library and bookstore shelves are filled with biographies of people who have survived incredible stories of loss. Those accounts will inspire and encourage you to greater heights. Forget the nightly television ritual and develop a new one—make some hot tea (winter) or lemonade (summer) and find companionship in a story of hope. You will be amazed at what it will do for you.

2. ***Don't forget the good things going on all around you.*** It's easy to count our problems and forget our blessings. I am reminded of a familiar hymn, *"Count Your Many Blessings . . ."* Not count your few, but your *many.* Something tells me you have much to be thankful for.

3. ***Give yourself permission to enlarge your world.*** Read the daily newspaper to see what is transpiring on both the local and national scene. Think about issues that are in the news. Get back up to speed and inject current events into conversation. It's okay.

4. ***Eat out.*** Not all the time but some of the time. It's depressing to eat alone. If you can't find anyone with whom to eat, grab that book you're reading (see above) and make it your companion. Chances are, however, if you have a circle of friends at church or in the neighborhood, there may be others who would enjoy your company as you would enjoy theirs. Beware: they may be stuck, too. (That's when you can recommend this book.)

5. ***Embrace the power of prayer.*** Talk to God out loud. Not only mention your personal struggles but work to enlarge your prayer life to include others who are hurting. Pray for them and then tell them you have lifted them up before the throne. They will be appreciative and you will have taken a small step toward your own recovery.

It's a long journey. As a good friend often tells me, "It's all about progress, not perfection." And you take one step at a time. You work through denial. You work through anger. The fog of depression (although everyone has their days) begins to lift. Acceptance comes and . . . healing begins.

Climb on, my friend. You're making progress.

Chapter 9

❊❊❊

My Greatest Fear

DAVID

I stood in line at the convenience store and waited to pay for my gas purchase. It was mid-afternoon, about a week-and-a-half after Adam died. I hadn't yet returned to work, but planned to on the following Monday. The wounds from his death were still imminently fresh, and I felt zombie-like as I waited to take my turn behind a couple of other people. When I stepped to the counter and handed money to the cashier, that's when I saw it, in a rack with other newspapers by the door as you exit the store: *Baseball Weekly.*

Adam was an avid baseball fan, a love he learned from me. He played PeeWee and Little League as a youngster—I was his coach—and he kept up with his favorite teams and players. But he was a fan like I never was. After he quit playing the game, he studied it. He traveled during the summer with friends to visit different ballparks across the country because he wanted to experience them firsthand—and see baseball games. He watched ESPN's *Baseball Tonight* every night, and had the uncanny ability to tell you who played every position on every team in the majors. I know because I questioned him—frequently—just to see if he could do it. He collected cards by the thousands and traded them regularly. He bought *Beckett's Baseball Card Monthly*, a monthly catalogue of every baseball card available—before such information was really available online—and regularly pored through it to keep up with the value of the cards he had and the ones he wanted. He knew the standings in each league and division, knew what kind of year each player was having and who the up-and-coming prospects were. And he read *Baseball Weekly*. It was usually spread on the floor of his bedroom, with his baseball cards, *Beckett's,* and the notes and lists that he kept.

I stared at the *Baseball Weekly* as I exited the store. My mind was racing. As I walked to my car that sunny afternoon, nearly two weeks after Adam's accident, it hit me for the very first time: Adam would never coach a baseball team. I would never hear him yell instructions across the field to his team like I did to his. He would never know the joy of seeing his own children play the game he loved so much. Then another lightning bolt hit me, again for the first time: Adam would never have children! I would never see grandchildren from him. Shaken, I sat down in my car, closed the door behind me, placed my face in my hands, and cried.

The New Horizon

I hate to tell you this—perhaps you know it already—but you'll have revelation moments like that, moments that sweep over you like an ocean wave, and beat you back down to the beginning, where you feel like you're starting all over again. Don't fret. It's going to be like that for a little while. You're adjusting to the new and different look of the horizon of your future.

A death in your immediate family changes your life so dramatically. That is especially so when your child dies because it turns the natural order of things upside down. Frankly, I expected to bury my father, and I did in April 1999. I expect that one day I'll bury my mother, who is now approaching ninety years old. I expect that I may bury one or both of my brothers, and I expected that I might even bury my wife—one of us had to die first. Not surprisingly, however, I never, ever, expected to see my son in a box. Every parent knows it's possible, but no parent has it on their list of expectations. After Adam died, I simply concluded that "normal" didn't exist for us anymore. And it didn't. Everything had changed. Even our identity—as the parents of *three* sons—seemed different.

Wilson introduced you earlier to Debbie Reeves, a woman from Alabama who lost her husband to divorce, and then ten months later, lost her precious middle son, Gabriel, a high school sophomore, in an auto accident. She knows the awful pain of grief and sorrow, and how it feels when the landscape of your life changes so dramatically and permanently. She was scarcely beginning to heal from the ravages of divorce and its impact on her and her sons, when Gabriel's untimely death struck another blow.

Debbie describes her reaction to the reality of a different future like none I've ever heard. "I grieved," she says, "for the life I'd lost, the one I dreamed about, the one I was supposed to have, the one I would never have. My cottage dream of home and family had taken a turn and would never be the same." In other words, she grieved not only for the loss of her son and family as she knew it, but she grieved loss of the vision she had of life as it was to be, as she expected it to be, a life now lost. Doesn't that describe how we all grieve at some point in time? It does for me.

As I began to visualize how things would be different without Adam, I looked ahead to certain events in the future with a special kind of dread because they were not going to be what I expected them to be. As odd as it may sound, one of the first I thought of was his ten-year high school class reunion. I knew his old friends would gather to laugh and celebrate the foibles of growing up, and I also knew that even though I wouldn't be present at that event, his name would be read aloud as one of the ones no longer "with us." I knew because at my high school reunions—and every high school reunion of which I'm aware—they did, and do, the very same thing. Typically, when the names of the deceased are read at a class reunion, you think back about those people for a sad moment, but you know that life goes on for you, that you have your own job, your own career, your own family, your own life, and you can't crowd it too much with the memory of others long past gone. Imagining *my* son's name being read for his memory was nauseating and repugnant to me. It reinforced that he was gone and would not come back.

The thought of Adam's ten-year reunion—without him present—exposed my great fear that he would be forgotten, and that as others went on with their lives, Adam's memory would simply eventually fade away. In one moment I could picture my son laughing and reminiscing with his high school friends, and in the next I had to erase it as an event that would never occur. It was as if all the hopes and dreams I had stored up for him just disappeared, like steam over a boiling pot. I didn't want that to happen, and frankly, I suspect that no parent does. Time had stopped for my Adam, but it moves on for everyone else.

The Cemetery Overcoat

Perhaps our fear that Adam's memory would fade best evidenced itself at the cemetery where he's buried. We placed a large stone at his grave and tended it with flowers and plants. We decorated it with flags from Duke and Indiana Universities, his two favorite schools, and periodically watered the grass over his grave during the hot Kentucky summers to keep it alive. When different holidays rolled around, we usually did something special. The first two Halloweens after his death, Kyle painted pumpkins with the familiar logos of the New York Mets and Duke Blue Devils, because Adam would have been excited about them. We took balloons on his birthday and tried to make sure that his grave had seasonal colors.

Of course, there is nothing wrong with any of those things, and most everyone—not all, but many—who experience loss, do something similar to insure that the memory of their loved one is honored. That is not to say it is good or bad, but that it is something we do. You may do it, too. Frankly, experience has taught me that it is part of the process of letting go.

I think of Adam or Debbie every day, and their memory is in a sweet place in my mind. Frequent trips to the cemetery, however, are no longer the healthiest thing for me to do. I needed to go there frequently at first, especially after Adam died—Debbie and I both did. The cemetery was the last place I left him, and it drew me like a magnet to fill the void for his absence.

The tradeoff is that you can get stuck in the time warp and you revisit the horror of loss over and over. Sorrow, especially for your child, is like a horrible dungeon and is an awful, awful place to be. Time and experience have taught me that it's hard (at least it was for me) to move forward from grief, with my mind and feet planted in the moment of tragedy and loss. Grief wears on you like a heavy overcoat, and eventually you have to begin to take it off if you want to move on. I visit the cemetery every now and then to honor Adam's and Debbie's memories, but if I spend too much time there, the names and dates on their headstones take me back to a place I don't want to be. You have to wean yourself from it at your own pace.

I know a lady from Massachusetts whose seventeen-year-old daughter hung herself one day after she received a rejection letter from a nursing school. When my friend came home from work that afternoon, she found her daughter hanging in a stairwell that went to the cellar. I can't imagine the horror. That was in the mid-1960s. She told me several years ago that for two years after her daughter's death, she visited the cemetery and sat at her daughter's grave in a vigil for several hours every day. She didn't miss a day. Finally after two years, she was still grieving and hurting like she had at the beginning, and realized that she had to stop going to the gravesite so she could move on and lift herself out of the valley. It's a hard thing for a parent (and even a spouse, but especially a parent) to do. She's in her eighties now and still hurts for the loss of her daughter. She always will even though it was forty years ago. But she moved to Maine in the 1970s, and it's been years since she visited that gravesite.

After she told me about how she dealt with it, I started to visit Adam's grave with less and less frequency, and it helped me emotionally in a noticeable way. I began to accept that Adam wasn't coming with me, and I had to adjust to life without him. It didn't mean I loved him less, but it helped me start to move on—to remember the sweet things and leave the dark memories behind.

A Difficult Move

It is extraordinarily difficult to move on through life and leave one of your children behind. Only a parent who has lost a child can know what it's like. What do you do with their belongings—the baby clothes, the handprints from kindergarten, the trophies and awards, the certificates and school diplomas? Under ordinary circumstances, parents keep such things for their kids until they have a home of their own so they can keep their childhood mementos themselves. Eventually, they'll pass down their history and precious keepsakes along to their children until at some point someday someone may throw it all away. Significantly, however, *you* are not the one to do it. In *your* vision of the future, your child and the reminders of their—and your—past are intact. But when your child dies, there's no one to whom you can pass those things, unless it's another child or, perhaps, a friend or other relative, who may already have plenty to keep. So, what do you do?

Those decisions were difficult for us. When I first began to think of removing Adam's things, I wondered if others might think I didn't care for him. Of course, our friends and family knew how we loved him and they saw us grieve. Those who truly care for you will not judge you harshly if you wish to remove your child's belongings as part of your healing process. At some point in time, they will expect you to do it, and will be happy that you are recovering. Adam's loss taught me that I needed to wean myself from an environment saturated with constant reminders of his death. No amount of mementos or keepsakes would bring him back; instead, they would heap sorrow upon sorrow.

Worse yet, though, was that I felt that in order to love him as I always did I had to leave his things as they were. Of course, that wasn't true, and I came to realize that. I will always love him, but I had to realize that I could not and cannot love him in the same, physical way anymore. That is a difficult adjustment for a parent.

Once again, however, time and distance from Adam's death helped me see that with a more objective perspective. Death, especially when you're inexperienced with it, leaves you clawing for any and every memory of your loved one, and it may for a time distort your vision. You need not hurry with your decisions. If you are unsure about what to do with clothing or belongings, it doesn't hurt to wait a little longer before you decide what to do. You'll know when you're ready.

When Adam died, Debbie wouldn't (or couldn't) alter anything about his closet. Kyle moved into his room and changed a few things to make it his, but Adam's closet remained untouched. His scent was in his clothes, and his baseball card and other collections filled his closet from floor to ceiling. As a result, it was a lingering part of Adam that she couldn't let go. It was, I suspect, a way she could keep a certain part of our lives with him the same. Fortunately, we could simply close the closet door. It was inconvenient for Kyle, but he was okay with it.

Shortly before she died, Debbie was methodically going through our house doing a *Trading Spaces* makeover, room by room. I suggested we clean out Adam's closet, but she said she wasn't "quite ready yet." Personally, as much as I missed him I didn't want to keep a shrine in his room—it had been nearly five years—but if she wasn't ready to remove it, who better than me could understand her wish to wait? As it turned out, Adam's closet never changed for her. She died before we did anything to it.

Her closet—our closet—however, changed shortly after she died. The first weekend after her funeral, Debbie's sister and I removed all of her clothes and belongings, except for a single blue blouse Debbie especially liked. I kept it because I could picture her smile as she wore it. But I needed to clean the closet; it was my closet, too; I used it everyday; and I felt it was healthiest for me to clean it out.

I was glad I did. Later, when I sold the house we had shared for sixteen years, I had to clean out Adam's closet and all the toys and stuff of his childhood years. It was an *extraordinarily* emotional and painful experience. I was forced to revisit the grief of his loss all over again.

Of course, I still kept some of the things that were important to him and to us, but we (Kyle, Colin, and I) "let go" of much of the clutter and items that were of no real value to us. We didn't keep every memory, but we kept the ones that counted. Very likely, there are still things that need to be sold, given to others, or simply discarded. But I will make those decisions when and if I have to, and it will be easier since I've done the hard part. For now, the job is finished.

As difficult as it was, I came to terms with the fact that moving his treasures, giving away his clothing, or discarding things that were important to him but to no one else (like a newspaper article about the New York Mets winning the 1986 World Series) did not mean that we had forgotten him.

Debbie Reeves, who I mentioned earlier, approached those decisions a little differently—because she had no choice. After her divorce, she was left with few photos from her children's early years because her ex-husband had selfishly taken all of them (except for one photo album he could not find), and he refused to obey a court order to divide them. When Gabriel died, his oldest brother, Michael, his cousin, Lee, who was like a brother, and several other friends went through Gabriel's personal items and kept small things that were important to each of them. Debbie explained that when Michael told her what they had done, she was unsure how she felt because they went through his things before she had had a chance to even think about it. But after some reflection, she realized that they were grieving, too, and that was their way to connect to Gabriel's memory.

Later, family and friends pored through their collections of old photographs to find pictures of Debbie's children, and she placed all three of her sons' keepsakes and photos in her hope chest—a large trunk she'd had since she was in junior high school. The size of the trunk required her to pare down the number of items she kept to things that were truly special, but she always has it available to go through when she feels like a trip down memory lane.

Each person who experiences loss has to work through these issues in their own way and own time—including you. That won't make your job any easier, but you need to know that others have plowed this ground too, and worked through the difficult decisions that you face.

When I shared with Debbie Reeves my concern that memory of Adam might fade, she expressed no real fear that Gabriel would be forgotten. Instead, she explained how she frequently shared stories about Gabriel's life to others in the hope that they would be encouraged by the kind of life he led, particularly since he died so young. She is regularly reminded of the declaration in Hebrews 11:4: "By faith he still speaks even though he is dead." She hopes Gabriel's life speaks to help others in the very same way.

Frankly, I think that the fear I felt that Adam might be forgotten, and Debbie Reeves' hope for Gabriel's memory to help others, both express the same thing in a different way. We both want our children's lives to have counted for something, to have had a positive influence on others, and have meaning. It helps to make sense of it all. Perhaps you feel the same way. Whatever the case, we had to eventually accept the inalterable changes we faced in our futures, and you do, too. Time—lots of it—is an important ingredient in that process. It can't be hurried along. Do not be impatient. Don't immerse yourself in death, but wean yourself from it at your pace, and gradually the healing will come.

As we tried to adjust to the changes we faced after Adam died, the saying in our house was that there was a "new normal." So it is with everyone who faces loss. Adam's classmates and his especially close friends have been wonderful about keeping in touch with us about the changes in their lives—getting married, having children, and other significant events—but when I hear of their successes, it's hard not to think about what might have been.

Other Fears

Maybe you're saying, "Those fears are not my fears." Maybe not. Here are some others. Perhaps you'll recognize one or more of them.

It can happen again. Yes, it can. I think about Job. Despite the great blessings he received from God with ten more children and twice as much wealth as before, I suspect that he went to his grave with a hole in his heart for his ten children who died. As parents, we know it *can* happen again, but you can't go through life gripped in fear. If that is how you truly feel, then change your life and relationship to God so you don't live in fear, but live in hope! (see 1 John 3:18 and Heb. 2:14–15). Then work to help effect those same changes in the lives of your children and others you love. It takes time and hard work, but it can happen.

I'll never be happy again. Are you convinced that happiness is out of reach, and you'll never have it again? I understand feeling that way, because for me, "normal" didn't exist anymore. But I will tell you standing on this side and this distance from tragedy and loss, that that kind of "fear" is *not* reality. You can and will be happy again, but it takes time and work and trust. Jesus declared: "all things are possible with God" (Mark 10:27). Do you believe Him? Paul wrote: "I can do everything through Him who gives me strength" (Phil. 4:13). This is not some deal you do alone. Anchor yourself with Scripture.

My friend Morris, a solo practitioner CPA, was diagnosed with cancer a number of years ago. He went through his therapeutic regimen, lost his hair and his strength, and battled his cancer with a fierce and competitive attitude. He explained that when he was sick, he could have spent the day in his pajamas in bed, wallowing in the dreariness of an awful, debilitating disease. But instead, no matter how bad he felt, he got up every morning, put on his shirt and tie and went to his office to work. He realized that before he could overcome the physical test of his disease, he had to overcome the mental and emotional challenges he faced. So he got up and did something about it everyday. Though there may be differences in the kinds of grief you face and Morris faced, the need to exercise the mental toughness to lift yourself is the same.

Wilson and Julie have a poster in their house that has a saying on it, the principle of which applies here: "There's not an elevator to success. You have to take the stairs." That saying was never truer than when applied to healing and happiness from grief and sorrow. You may feel like you're stuck and making no progress, and you're waiting for the Silver Bullet Train to shoot you to happiness. How long have you been stuck here? Has it been long enough? Don't be over-anxious. Has it been too long? If you feel mired in grief and depression, jump-start yourself! Get up, get dressed, open the shades and let in the light of a new day. Go back and re-read the last two chapters. Develop a greater dependence and trust in God. Find others to help who are hurting. Take affirmative steps to change things—even the little things—in your life that are weighing you down with sorrow. Remember you are taking the stairs, and it takes time, but eventually you'll get to where you want to go emotionally, and happiness is waiting for you there.

My family won't recover from this experience in a healthy way. I can understand how this could be a real fear. You worry that despite what you do to recover and deal with your grief in a healthy way, you can't ensure that your family will do the same thing. So you add to your burdens the worry that grief and sorrow could claim additional "victims" from the people you love.

You can't ensure how other people will react to tragedy. In fact, you probably didn't know how you'd react yourself until you walked a mile in these shoes. What you can do to help others is encourage them and assist them as you recognize their needs. Pray for the Lord to lift the heavy weight of anguish from them, and pray that you have wisdom in the way you respond to them. Give it to God—and don't give up on Him or them. Just as you trust Him to help you, trust Him to help them, and encourage them to trust Him in the same way. There's no substitute for reliance on God. This is not a job that's too big for Him.

There may be some other fear I haven't mentioned that has crossed your mind, or plagues you now. If so, I wish there were something I could say, or some encouragement I could give you. Remember this, however: whatever fear or challenge you face, it will help resolve with time and reliance on God.

Chapter 10

Holidays—and Other Bad Days

WILSON

"John Grisham wrote a story called Skipping Christmas.
I wish."
—Divorced Dad

"Holidays are the saddest time for me."
—Eight-year-old boy

Nightmare. Turmoil. Absolute dread. Stress. Painful. An eye-rolling accident waiting to happen—these and more are words that have been used by the divorced to describe that wonderful time of year from Thanksgiving to New Year's. With the quick pound of a judge's gavel, the holidays approach like an ominous cloud that forms on the horizon, reminding you that your family will no longer be the same (as if you needed the extra reminder).

Every family experiences stress around the holidays. We all tend to spend too much, eat too much, and cram too many activities into overloaded lives. Add a divorce and children into the equation and holiday stress is magnified a hundred fold. Divorced parents must attempt to communicate with an even greater diplomacy, juggle schedules, negotiate multiple dinners, arrange holiday travel, appease extended family, deal with the pain of separation from children, and face the gargantuan task of avoiding competition gift-giving. And, as if that were not enough, The Ghosts of Holidays Past keep raising their nostalgic heads, reminding you of the way it used to be.

The horrible aftermath of both death and divorce come home for the holidays and the dread faced by those struggling with either is similar. While I can speak to the former, and David to the latter, please be advised that there is no magic wand to be waved that will remove the pain or make the nasty go away regardless of the blackness of your grief. Jesus said each must bear his own cross—and at year's end it takes on even extra weight.

Holly and Melancholy

One of the hardest tasks faced by those living in the wake of either death or divorce is pretending to carry on previous family traditions with a sense of normalcy—when you know there isn't any. Just the thought of putting up the Christmas tree, setting out decorations, and shopping for gifts filled me with a dread never before experienced. My first Christmas as a single dad of three was awful. My second Christmas was better—Julie had entered my life and family—but it was still a chore. She is quick to remind me that when we began to hang ornaments on the tree, I went upstairs and disappeared. I don't remember. But she does. For some reason (probably painful) I have blocked it out of my mind.

What I have never blocked out is the memory of watching three children drive away, or worse—board an airplane together—and leave me standing, buried under an avalanche of December tears. I know. Dads aren't supposed to cry. Maybe not, but I did.

As hard as Christmas was, Thanksgiving was even worse.

Every family is different but Thanksgiving has always been at the top of my list for family holidays. While much about Christmas has come to be immersed in the sham of commercialism, Thanksgiving is still about hearth and home, friends and family. At least for us. And while it doesn't matter to me whether we open gifts on Christmas Eve, Christmas day, before or beyond, Thanksgiving is pretty solid on the calendar. It happens on the fourth Thursday of November. Always. And the children were either with me or they weren't. Like most visitation schedules, Thanksgiving alternated and that meant—even years with dad, odd years with mom.

It was the bluest day of the year.

It is heartbreaking to gather with family—parents, siblings, nieces, nephews, cousins, and the rest of the family and do so without your own children. And even though you know they are coming home in a few days and also know that next year will be *your* holiday, for some nostalgic reason you realize the present-day emptiness and feel they have missed something very important. And so have you.

Just the fact that you are flying solo (as in "so low") this holiday is the elephant in the room everyone tries to avoid. No one wishes to upset you or say the wrong thing and invariably someone does. So, you swallow it and smile—all the while feeling the empty sickness in the pit of your soul.

Holidays magnify the pain. And when you are left alone on those days—including birthdays, Easter, and any other days that are special to you and your children—you have to fight with everything you have to not pull both curtains and covers and hibernate in a cave of self-pity for the duration. Sometimes you lose that battle.

Surviving

Little redheaded Annie smiles and sings, "The sun will come out tomorrow . . ." I've read a lot of articles and books with qualified psychologists suggesting ways to fight through the holidays, but that cute kid beats them all. The sun will come out tomorrow—or at least the next day. The holidays will come and go and, in spite of the stress, you will survive. Turkey won't look appetizing for the next three months, fake Christmas trees go back into the attic, and anything that resembles the holiday season disappears into the abyss of out-of-sight, out-of-mind. Finally.

It's hard to see that, however, when you're alone and other families seem so full of love and laughter.

Okay, enough of the gray slush. If you've been in it, you already know how bad it is. If not, then it is impossible for me, David, or anyone else to explain. It's a you-have-to-have-been-there/done-that to understand. And while the pain is bad, it can be lessened.

Here are some commonsense things you can learn on my dime. They aren't cure-alls, or psychobabble, and not all will work for everyone. But they contain lessons I have learned (and some the hard way) that may help you muddle through and come out on top a survivor. Some may hit you harder than others, while a few may not hit you at all. Ready, set . . .

Ten Ways to Ease the Pain

1. *Don't try and recreate holidays past.* You can't. Things are different now and the sooner you accept reality the better off you and everyone else around you will be. That doesn't mean you can't maintain certain traditions—you should. In fact, drastic wholesale changes are counterproductive to your mental health. Keep some; change others. You may want to eat out instead of in. Or change menus. Put the Christmas tree up in another room . . . buy additional decorations . . . mix new holiday music in with the old . . . Do whatever will help you cope.

After Julie entered our world, we began two new family traditions. First, each year we went ornament shopping and allowed the children to each purchase one new ornament. It was a lot of fun—especially as the years rolled along and we decorated the tree with their new imaginative ornaments. And some were quite imaginative! But that was okay—it not only fit who they were that year but provided a few laughs in years to come. "I can't believe I chose that one . . ." has been echoed more than once. An added feature to this new tradition is that when one of them gets married and leaves the nest, their ornaments go with them. And then, hopefully, as they trim their tree, it will bring back for them some fond memories and a smile or two from their growing-up years.

The second new tradition was the beginning of a Christmas memory book, including a family picture from the year, along with the family Christmas card we mailed to friends. There is a page to recreate the events of the year and it becomes a holiday highlight not only to record the memorable happenings of the year completed but . . . a chance to relive years past. Years have a way of blurring time and events, but our Christmas memory book enables us to live again all the funny and sad and in-between events of our family. Our daughter and family have begun their own memory book that I hope they will treasure as much as we do ours.

The point is . . . just because you have experienced a life-shattering divorce, doesn't mean that you can't pick up the big chunks of glass and re-glue. Even the holidays—as much as they anchor us to the past—can, if we let them, be a bridge to tomorrow. Keep a few old traditions but start some new ones. Go for it!

2. *Give yourself a break.* I'm going to go out on a great big limb and suggest that . . . you're not perfect. Me neither. Whoa! I hope you're okay with that admission/confession. We make mistakes. It's not like most of us have been down this path before. You can read all the dos and don'ts written by qualified doctors and lawyers about the whats and what nots of how you should conduct yourself around your kids during the holidays—and you'll still mess up occasionally.

For example . . .
- *You know* you cannot buy their love, but you give in to an extra gift . . .
- *You know* you should see them off without bursting into tears, but try as hard as you can to hold back the flood gates . . .
- *You know* you should smile when they excitedly tell you about what mom/dad bought them or where mom/dad took them, but inside you are boiling . . .
- *You know* you should get over it and move on, but every time you see other families . . .

Listen here, Superman or Wonder Woman—you are neither. You will make mistakes, stumble, and violate all the rules. Give yourself permission . . . *to be normal.* That doesn't mean you approve of mistakes; it just means that you acknowledge that you make them and resolve to learn from them. Quit being so hard on yourself. It will get better and you will do better—in time.

3. *Make your own special plans.* "Home Alone" makes for a great movie but doesn't do much to beat the holiday blues. Get with someone. Look

for those at church or among neighbors and friends who may also be in your predicament and plan a special dinner or evening out. Sometimes we think that we're the only ones "Home Alone" when in fact there are probably many within the realm of our acquaintance circle suffering the same painful experience. Make plans. If the children are away for a few days, take a road-trip to visit a friend. If you're worried about being a burden upon their holiday, then go the day after. Plan something fun that you can look forward to with some measure of enthusiasm. If nothing else, busyness will help you pass the time.

4. *Talk to your children.* Make sure they know "the schedule" and where they will be and when. Other than opening gifts on Christmas morning, they don't like surprises any more than do you. But whatever you do, it is supremely important that you do not burden them with the responsibility of your unhappiness. Do not tell your child that you will be miserable, lonely, in tears, and completely depressed while they are with the other parent (even if all of the above are true). They don't need to know that. Tell them that you will miss them and that you'll be together again very soon. Then when you're sure they are asleep, grab the tissues and have a good cry. (If you're a frustrated dad, go out into the garage and hammer on something. But not too loudly).

5. *Give yourself an extra gift.* The end of a relationship doesn't mean that you don't deserve a little extra from Santa. Buy something you need or have put off and then go home, wrap it, put "From Santa" on the tag, and slip it under the tree. If nothing else, you'll smile every time you walk past and if you tell a friend or two about what you've done, they'll smile, too. There can be some sparkles of fun even in the midst of grief.

6. *Help your child buy a gift for the other parent.* (I didn't say these were easy suggestions . . .) One of the hardest things I ever did was take children shopping and make sure they had a gift for the other parent. As they grew older and more independent, they were able to do it themselves (yeah!), but for a time it was important for me to help them. Or at least I thought so. I had to keep telling myself: "This gift

is not from me, it is from my child." I tried to focus on the joy of the child as the giver rather than the parent receiving. I said *I tried . . .* I didn't say I always succeeded. And whether or not the good deed is ever reciprocated (don't expect it), and whether or not your child will even remember you doing this (probably not), you will know you did the right thing. The Lord will reward.

7. *Stop the competition.* This is probably the biggest gripe of the divorced custodial parent. The "Disney-World Parent" (noncustodial) seems to provide the biggest and most lavish gifts—often as a means to compensate for the guilt of their leaving. Remember the song: *Can't Buy Me Love?* Money won't buy love for your kids either. That's hard to see at the moment they're telling you about the cool ski trip hosted by the other parent, or the expensive new techno gadget they've been asking you for but which was outside of your price range. Try (try very, very hard!) to remember that you will not fail your child, nor will they grow up loving the other parent more if you live within your means. The expensive fun stuff will fade while the memories of a parent who loved them and gave them what they needed the most—unconditional love—will rise to the top and they will not forget. Trying to win some kind of undefined competition is a major lose-lose. Don't go there.

8. *Stick to the parenting plan or visitation schedule.* If the other parent refuses to cooperate, there isn't much you can do. Your ex-spouse knows which buttons to push and how far, and may leave you frustrated and feeling helpless. You aren't. Stay calm. A measured and well-thought-out response is favored over a knee-jerk reaction. If the situation gets too far out of bounds or happens repeatedly, seek the counsel of your lawyer. This doesn't mean that parents can't move outside the boundaries of "the schedule" if both agree to a fair arrangement, and it's good to be flexible if you can. But regardless of what the other parent does, you do the right and honorable thing. Keep your word and do what you said you would do. It's what you would expect from your children, so lead the way by example.

9. *Give your child permission to love the other parent.* It doesn't mean you agree with or approve of the behavior of your former spouse, but it does mean that you understand the need your child has to love both mom and dad. The actions of the other parent are not your fault nor are they the fault of your child. Regardless of what he/she has done, they are still a father/mother to your child. All of which means, the best gift you can give your child is permission to love the other parent.

WARNING: This may be the hardest test of all! It will definitely take time and you may not be there yet. It is especially difficult when the other parent parades their significant other or newfound "love" in front of you and you're forced to "deal with it." The temptation to cast your disdain for their behavior, if not careful, will cause you to cross the line and cast disdain toward them as a person/parent. Take a deep and long breath and watch your words, for they tend to travel with your children. "Cast your anxiety upon the Lord"—not the kids. In time you will be able to help them understand what true love is; that it is deeper than words and is, in fact, a decision of the will fulfilled in a life of commitment. The more you help them understand this truth, the more likely they will be to cement future relationships that they may have. In the meantime, children will love their mom/dad regardless of what they have done. It is essential that you understand that. Certainly you as the adult comprehend the ramifications of wrong behavior, but your children may not. At least not now. Give it time. Give them time. Give yourself time. Most of all, give God time to work on helping your children understand.

10. *Make alone time fun and productive.* Try as you might, you may face some time when you are alone over the holidays, have no plans, and the day looms long and empty. Even then there are things you can do to pass the day and be productive. It doesn't have to be earth-shattering and spectacular. What works for you may not work for another. But what works for you is . . . *what works for you.* I suggest:

- rent a movie(s), pop some corn, and watch what *you* want to see
- buy a special meal to eat at home
- lose yourself in a good book that you can't put down

- take a one hour beauty bath with music and candles (for the ladies)
- tackle a home project you've been wanting to do (for the guys)
- organize something (my wife says I do that when I'm frustrated)
- stay in bed and watch TV (there's no law against it)
- write thank-you notes to people who have been kind to you and the kids
- take a long walk and listen to music
- read Psalm 31 slowly, let it penetrate your soul, then bow and talk to God.

> Be gracious to me, O Lord, for I am in distress;
> My eye is wasted away from my grief, my soul and my body also.
> For my life is spent with sorrow, and my years with a sigh . . .
> But as for me, I trust in Thee, O Lord,
> I say, "Thou art my God."
> My times are in Thy hand;
> Deliver me from the hand of my enemies and from those who persecute me.
> Make Thy face to shine upon Thy servant;
> Save me in Thy lovingkindness . . .
> How great is Thy goodness,
> Which Thou hast stored up for those who fear Thee . . .
> Thou dost hide them in the secret place of Thy presence . . .
> Be strong, and let your heart take courage,
> All you who hope in the Lord.
> —Psalm 31:9–10a,14–16,19a,20a,24

Annie is right! You *can* get through a holiday alone and the sun *will* come out tomorrow. Each year gets better. It may be hard to grasp the truth of that now but in time you will. Please remember that holidays, as memorable as they are, are single-day events in a very long calendar year. As hard as it is, try to see the bigger picture.

Holidays aren't the only tough days. I think David has an angle or two you need to hear about . . .

DAVID

Although it seemed like every day was a bad day after Adam died, the first "real" holiday to roll around was Thanksgiving. Of course, that doesn't count Halloween, which was typically a family time for our family, when the boys and I always carved a jack-o-lantern for our front porch. Since Adam would have otherwise been away at IU, however, it really didn't change what we'd ordinarily do.

On Thanksgiving, though, we did everything the way we always had and gathered with Debbie's family at her mother's home in Owensboro, Kentucky. Despite the presence of nearly twenty people, all I can say is that Adam, the oldest grandchild, was *noticeably* absent, and the entire thing was a sad, teary event. We couldn't finish our Thanksgiving prayer without crying. We were only two months past his death, and the wounds were fresh for us all.

Debbie and I decided that we would do something entirely different for Christmas. After we finished our obligatory trips to visit family, we planned to leave immediately to go to Florida and vacation in an entirely different environment and climate. During the October fall break period, Debbie and her sister had gone to Destin, Florida for a week—a favorite vacation spot for our family—and it had been a welcome respite for her. Consequently, she thought it may work for us and the boys in the same way.

Since our boys are theme park enthusiasts, we decided to spend the week at Universal Studios in Orlando, where the weather, rides, and activities would entertain us and divert our attention from our hurting hearts. Of course, the New Year's celebration was also supposed to be exceptional because the calendar would turn to 2000. If I had to do it all over again, I would do the same thing. But I can tell you in advance that nothing will really divert your attention from your hurting heart.

Even though we were excited to take the trip together, we all knew why we were doing it, and honestly, a cloud hung over the holidays. Immediately after church on Sunday morning, December 26, we drove to Nashville. My brother had made arrangements for us to have tickets to great seats at a Tennessee Titans play-off game, and from there we went to the airport to catch our flight. When we arrived in

Orlando, we rented a car, ate supper, and made our way to our hotel. After we settled in, we decided to go down to the hotel restaurant and get dessert—something special to finish the day—so we could start "having fun" the next morning.

The restaurant host asked, "How many?" and I quietly said, "Four," which was itself a reminder that Adam wasn't with us. The host led us to a round table in the corner of the room, a table, it appeared, which usually sat six. On this night, however, *five* chairs were positioned around it. Debbie and I both looked at the chair in stunned silence. Tears still well up in my eyes when I recall it.

"Is this okay?" our host asked.

"Thank you," I replied, and we sat down.

I cannot recall for certain, but I believe it was Kyle who said, "Can you believe it?" Of course, we ordered our dessert and finished the evening, but it goes without saying that "Adam's chair" was foremost in our minds.

We enjoyed our week. It *was* a great distraction. But no matter what we did, we always asked ourselves, "Wouldn't Adam have loved this?" Even now, when I look at photos from that vacation, I specifically notice that Adam is absent from them. One photo in particular was taken on December 31, 1999, the evening of the New Year's Eve fireworks celebration. Debbie had a pair of glittery "2000" faux glasses, and we asked someone to take our picture. Though the picture shows the four of us smiling, I can see we were hurting.

As the New Year's countdown approached that night, we found a spot from which to watch the fireworks display, and the park lights were darkened just minutes before it began. The clock clicked the final seconds toward midnight, and loudspeakers blared "three-two-one." At midnight's stroke, fireworks burst overhead, people cheered, and *Auld Lang Syne* rang out everywhere. It really was a sight, and symbolic to us—the end of the worst year of our lives and the start of a new year—a new beginning of sorts. But our hearts didn't feel the difference. As everyone counted "one!"—the last tick of 1999—Debbie and I looked at each other. We said "Happy New Year" to each other, kissed quickly, embraced as tightly as we could, and cried like babies. We shook in each other's arms for what seemed like a full minute. I cannot write it now without crying. We missed our son so much. Not even a new year could take our grief away.

And it won't take away yours. As each holiday occurs, you will adjust. It will hurt, but you will adjust.

Experience has taught me that the first full year is the hardest. Just get through the first year. Every day on the calendar is a new one without your loved one, and until you've clicked off the first year, each experience cuts you like a new wound. Eventually, however, the first year will end. The second year will be difficult, but if you are trying to heal, it will be better.

For me, the anniversary of Adam's death is the worst day, and frankly, most everyone I've talked to who has lost children feels the same. I say that, however, nine years removed from the event. The first three Thanksgivings and Christmases after his accident were difficult times, and we almost had to make ourselves celebrate the holidays when, in our heart of hearts, we didn't want to.

His birthday comes and goes with its moment of melancholy, and the other holidays have their eventual moments of sadness. But we can find new ways to celebrate holidays and slowly but surely create new traditions, and that's what we tried to do. The anniversary of death, however, is always the worst, at least for me. I can feel it coming, like a dark, unsettling, emotional cloud approaching from the distance. When the month of September arrives, the cloud begins to gather, and it hovers closer and closer as September 19 draws near. But once it has passed, I feel better.

Is there a way to get past that day? I haven't found it yet, if there is. It's an ordinary day on the calendar like most every other day. There's not a football game (usually) and nobody else is taking off from work. I have the day marked on my calendar as "Adam's Day," and I don't work on that day—my way, in part, to honor his memory. I will buy flowers and decorate his grave, but I make a special effort not to make it a day of sadness.

Others may feel differently, you included, and various holidays may affect you in varying ways. But I believe time helps to heal the wounds we feel on those special days, and given enough time—so long as the date of death did not occur on or near the holiday period—we heal from the awful hurt of their absence. If the date of your loved one's death is near the holiday period, then you may have a special challenge during that time that others—except those of us who have walked a mile in your shoes—cannot fully understand.

My advice to everyone who has lost a child or a spouse is to change something about your traditions to make it new and different. If it's Christmas, exchange gifts in a different room. Get a different Christmas tree. Plan to go someplace. Help someone who is going through the same thing or has a different set of problems—such as a single mom, a homebound person, or someone who is sick. Turn your attention away from you and do not wallow in self-pity. It may be difficult at first, but try not to focus on what you *don't* have, and be thankful for what you *do* have. And trust God, who supplies everything we need at all times to do His work, whatever it may be (2 Cor. 9:8).

It took me a little while to learn that the holidays would improve, and I know from experience that it is true. While you are in the tumult of grief, and everywhere you look there is a memory or treasure that throws you back into that awful, sickening dungeon of sorrow, it may be difficult to see that, but give it time. They will get better.

Wilson gave some great suggestions of ways to get through the holidays, and while the divorced face a different set of challenges, some of his suggestions will be nonetheless helpful, even for the grieving. You may find lots of other suggestions available near the holiday period in books, newspapers, and online. For some, The Compassionate Friends is a helpful resource (www.compassionatefriends.org). Whatever the case, when you feel lonely and hurting, holiday period or not, remember this:

- Rely on the Lord
- Read scripture, especially those passages that remind us of God's promises
- Pray frequently
- Look for and help others who need encouragement from you, and
- Keep on keeping on.

Chapter 11

<hr>

"They'll Get Over It!"

WILSON

I could not believe what I was hearing. Personal rejection and the finality of a divorce demand was one thing, but a nonchalant shrug-of-the-shoulders response to the question, *Do you know what this will do to the kids?* was quite another. But the words that title this chapter were the very words I heard. They have burned themselves into my memory as if etched with a branding iron. I knew then the folly of those words. And I still do.

My children did not "get over it." No child does.

It is interesting to talk to the children of divorce and, while no two stories are exactly the same, there is a consistent pattern easily observed. Most children will tell you that the day their parents divorced was the day their childhood ended. Is it that traumatic? *Yes.*

In the book, *The Unexpected Legacy of Divorce* by psychologist Judith Wallerstein, psychology professor Julia M. Lewis, and *New York Times* science correspondent Sandra Blakeslee, researchers studied ninety-three children of divorce and followed them into adulthood. When the study was concluded, the children were between the ages of twenty-eight and forty-three. The findings were eye-opening. Previously, "experts" believed that the most stressful time for children comes in the immediate aftermath of a divorce. Wallerstein, Lewis, and Blakeslee found that post-divorce difficulties became even more severe when the

<hr>

children of divorce reached adulthood and began their own search for lasting commitment.

It's no surprise to me. And if you have seen children of divorce come of age while continuing to wrestle with their parent's failure, you've seen it, too.

Adult children of divorce often grow up terrified—terrified that they are going to fail in their marriage just like their parents. As a result, many don't know how to choose a spouse and often make hasty choices. Children of divorce are far more likely to marry before the age of twenty-five than those from intact families and . . . far more likely to divorce soon thereafter. The statistics present a very real and alarming picture.

Aren't Kids Resilient?

They are. Kids are amazingly elastic, equipped with adaptable buoyancy that protects them from life's bumps and bruises. I remember well Julie's warnings the day she left this dad in charge of watching/protecting Luke, our fourth and youngest, when he was two years old. "Make sure you keep the door to the basement closed!" she said before venturing out. "You bet!" was my reply as I glanced up and over the sports section of the paper. To this day I don't know how it happened (a lady in the community told us later what our realtor had failed to disclose—our house was haunted), but somehow the little guy found the door open and before I could stop him, he took the first step down the basement stairs. About the time I hit the door he hit bottom. And then I watched incredulously as he bounced up with a grin as broad as a Cheshire cat and said, "You comin'?" A tumble down an entire flight of stairs, a fall that would have put me in traction for months, didn't even faze him. By the way, I did tell his mother about the incident—*ten years later.* I figured there had to be some kind of statute of limitations for a dumb dad.

Resiliency, however, is not without limits.

The common misconception about children of divorce is that they will bounce back with little impact. Don't believe it. Most kids (even adult kids) will require some kind of support system to help them cope with the ongoing saga of divorce—*the gift that keeps on giving.* Theirs is a pain that sometimes isn't diagnosed or even understood until decades after their parents' breakup. And each child will react differently.

Some children grow up with a determined disposition to rise above and overcome. They will use good judgment in their choosing of a mate and they will work hard at maintaining a healthy marriage. They have seen the effects of marital disharmony and want no part of it. Yet even they will struggle quietly with some side effects of divorce. It is inevitable.

Others struggle more openly. While some marry too quickly, thinking it will erase the hurt of a broken home, others react in an opposite way—they are hesitant to commit to a relationship—fearful that the sins of parents will revisit the next generation and sabotage their relationships. Both approaches can result from divorce scars. Still other kids grow old but never grow *up*. They struggle to find themselves bouncing from job to job or from school to school, often reacting in immature, rebellious, and harmful ways. Another scar.

The problem is this: adults make unwarranted assumptions about our children "getting over it"—because we have to. It is the mechanism of selfish people seeking to justify adult wishes. To do so we must invent myths to soothe our conscience, all the while placing personal needs and perceived happiness before the emotional well-being of our children. We attempt to justify our selfish behavior with the flippant idea that kids are resilient or that time will heal all wounds. The truth is—selfish parents cannot face the fact that their willful choices hurt their children. If you do not believe they hurt, ask the adult children of divorce.

Two Myths

Myth #1 states that the children will be happier if I get out of this unhappy marriage. A happy mom/dad equals a happy child. What sounds like solid rationale is, in fact, a lie. Adults who think like this are usually projecting their own feelings onto their children. The adult wants personal happiness without the stigma that he/she is bringing pain to their children. The truth be known (except in extreme cases), kids want their parents to stay together even if mom and dad don't always get along. And they employ unique methods to communicate it.

My kids loved the Disney movie, *The Parent Trap* (and later its remake). They watched it again and again. And I watched it with them. It's the cute tale of twin sisters who formulated a plan to reunite their divorced parents—complete with drama, comedy, and, above all, a happy ending. Were my kids communicating a message through a movie? Sure they were—whether they realized it or not or could articulate it or not. All children want an intact home—their mom and dad to live together.

When you introduce a child to divorce, you alter every part of their life. Every part. And as hard as divorce is on the adults involved, compound that a hundred fold for children who cannot begin to understand.

Maybe what makes a child happy is not what we think. Did you ever consider that the key to the happiness of a child is stability—a predictable routine? A child's happiness comes from having the *same* two parents, living in the *same* house with the *same* toys in the *same* neighborhood with the *same* friends to play with, going to the *same* school, and the day-to-day consistency of sameness in all of those areas. You don't have to have a degree in child psychology to figure this out. Kids like and need routine. It is the key to their happiness and overall well-being.

The idea that a child's happiness depends on parental happiness becomes a crutch-excuse to justify the selfish behavior of one who has bailed and doesn't want to feel guilty for doing so.

Myth #2 believes that as long as parents handle the divorce in an amicable way, the children will be fine. The problem with this approach is that few divorces are amicable. Usually one or the other mishandles their emotions as one or the other feels betrayed. Try as we might, personal hurt trickles down to the children. And then something amazing happens—the non-betrayed parent who has walked away will usually place the blame on the betrayed spouse for being the one causing all the pain. *If you had handled this better, the children wouldn't be so sad . . .*

Have you ever been hit over the head with a baseball bat while the perpetrator asks incredulously, *Why don't you just get over it?* Really. Let's see if I've got this right—you hit me with a bat and my reaction is the problem? Huh? But divorce is like that. With amazing regularity and predictability, those who walk away have a knack for shifting the blame back upon the innocent.

Like the biblical story of the mother who was willing to divide the baby, the selfish often do not care about the fallout or the ones they hurt. And divorce hurts. It hurts the spouse who has been betrayed and it hurts the children who live in the fallout. There is no way around it and no way to sugarcoat it. But whatever you do, do not buy into the lie that once the legal proceedings are over, everyone will live happily ever after. That's called "a fairy tale."

Roots and Wings

"Divorce seems like a forever time when you're in it." Debbie Reeves said that the very first night Julie and I met her and introduced her to David (more about that later). We gathered around our kitchen table to talk about the very subject that translated itself into the book you are holding. I know what she meant. In divorce you feel absolutely powerless and the hurt you feel for your children can at times be overwhelming. You want so very badly to make the nasty go away. But it never goes away.

That's why I must give my children the two greatest gifts any parent could ever bestow: *roots* and *wings*. They must have *roots* of faith that seek deeper soil. They must see in me evidence of an uncompromising trust in a God who is my rock. How many times is that designation used of Him in Scripture? When Jesus concluded the greatest sermon ever preached, He ended with a story about a man who built his house upon the rock. "And the rain descended and the floods came, and the winds blew, and burst against that house; and yet it did not fall, for it had been founded upon the rock" (Matt. 7:26). If I want my children to have rock-like faith, then I must have it first. I must teach them to trust in God by showing them that I do. And little by little the roots of their faith begin to find their hold.

And they will need it. The rain will descend upon them, the floods will come, the winds will blow against their house . . . but it will stand. It will stand only because they have come to embrace the living Lord as their rock.

Two things will help you. 1) A local church that stands upon the Word and reinforces principles that you're seeking to instill at home will be an invaluable source to complement your task. 2) A family support system of grandparents, aunts, uncles, and cousins will likewise add strength to their roots. Utilize both.

At the same time I seek to give them roots, I must give them *wings*. I raise them up to let them go. And that's especially hard for divorced parents. Sometimes the divorced throw themselves into their children to the unhealthy point of making them codependent. It is as cruel a deed as was perpetrated by the parent who abandoned them. God has given me a duty as a parent—to give my children wings to fly and enable them to live independent and productive lives. Raising children is akin to flying a kite. If you hold the string too tight it cannot fly. On the other hand, if you let out too much and too soon, the kite cannot make it on its own and comes crashing down. But God gives wisdom to the parent who asks (James 1:5). Ask. Pray for heavenly guidance. You will need it and He will give it.

Years later, the pain of divorce, although lessened by time, will rear its ugly head again. You can count on it. There will be weddings and special occasions, grandchildren and graduations—and once again you will be forced to face the failure of a marriage. It will be painful for your children, too, even adult children. Times such as these are awkward beyond belief. But you will survive and so will they because you have given them the two things they need to live—roots and wings.

Both death and divorce leave you feeling powerless. To hug and hold a crying child when you know you cannot do anything to make the hurt go away is one of the most crushing of feelings. Yet it is then we must draw upon heaven's strength.

> I will lift up my eyes to the mountains; from whence shall my help come? My help comes from the Lord who made the heavens and the earth. He will not allow your foot to slip;

He who keeps you will not slumber. Behold, He who keeps Israel will neither slumber nor sleep.

—Psalm 122:1–4

Rest well in the peace that God is always near. And while there are some things that neither you nor your children may ever "get over," with His help you can move on and get past. David has taught me that . . .

DAVID

Will they get over it? That's a question every parent mulls, especially when our children are young. How is this death going to affect them, the family dynamic, their outlook on life, and most importantly, how God deals with His people?

When Adam died, Kyle was eighteen and a freshman in college. Colin was thirteen and an eighth grader. We had never faced this kind of adversity before. I was concerned not only for my sons, but for how tragedy would bear on our family. I feared that Adam's death could derail our family's faith and take us as "casualties" of our misfortune, and we openly discussed it in family moments. But the real weight of how my sons would react didn't truly bear on me until Debbie's coma and death—when death suddenly and selfishly engulfed us again, when the deep, painful wounds of tragedy were ripped open a second time, and when I feared questions of God's fairness would surely begin to surface.

Perhaps I was too preoccupied and immersed in my own grief when Adam died, but as I look back now, I should have better realized how closely my sons would watch me handle the crisis moments. Now that you're in the crisis, you should have the same awareness. That's not to say I would or could have done anything differently. Death puts you in a fog, and sometimes you can only get by a moment at a time.

I have a word picture I use to describe the impact Adam's death had on me. Imagine the mushroom cloud of an atomic blast, and picture in your mind's eye the expanding wave of destruction that explodes from its center across the landscape. When Adam died, I felt like I was behind the wave, totally and completely decimated—annihilated—emotionally, mentally, and physically. It left me feeling completely helpless. I struggled to make it through each day, and described earlier in this book how I managed to do it.

Debbie's death did not debilitate me the same way or for the same length of time, and I trust my children understand that. There could be a number of reasons why. Perhaps it was the difference between losing a child and losing a spouse. Perhaps my experience with Adam's death left me better prepared to cope with hers. Perhaps it would have been different had Debbie's death occurred first. Personally, I am more inclined to believe that it was the difference between losing a child and a spouse than anything else, but I can never say for sure. Others to whom I have spoken, who have walked in the same shoes, have expressed to me the same opinion even though their losses occurred in different order, but my "survey" is casual and in no way scientific.

About six months after Adam died, a friend of mind lost her husband. They had been married for fifty-three years, and although he was in his seventies, he was in good health, and his death was sudden and unexpected. I visited her the morning after he passed away, and remember how she wept for him as we sat at her kitchen table. "David," she said, "I know you lost your son, but how can I get over the death of my husband, my companion, for fifty-three years?"

They had had no children, and I knew that we could not compare losses. I could not understand her grief because I hadn't walked a mile in her shoes, although I could try to imagine in my mind how her loss might feel. She could not understand my grief because she couldn't truly comprehend a parent's love for his or her child. And, frankly, comparing losses is a waste of time. If we hurt, we hurt, and the goal is to help one another mourn and to heal.

Thankfully, however, my friend recovered, and some time later she married again, to a widower acquaintance. Joy replaced sadness that had seemed irrepressible, and she continues to be happy to this day.

I do not personally believe, however, that I can ever get past Adam's loss in the same way, or for that matter, can any parent who has suffered the loss of a child. If I had other children born to me, none would replace Adam or fill the hole in my heart that he left. That is not to imply that I could, in fact, replace Debbie.

It would be impossible. She and I shared a special history and memories that were unique to us. I do believe, however, that I can replace her *companionship* as my spouse, just as my friend did, and I believe the good Lord equips us to do that. After all, it was God who said, "*It is not good for man to be alone.*"

Since Adam's and Debbie's deaths affected me in different ways, I knew they affected my sons differently as well, and I was concerned about how to help my children through it. After all, they were innocent and vulnerable, and I would've given all I had and all I could borrow to save them from the experience. I just wanted to see them get through to the other side of grief with a healthy dependence on God and outlook on life.

Grief counselors and therapists may identify some obvious differences in children to help measure their respective needs during the grief process, such as gender, birth order, age, education, wisdom and experience, the relationship between the parent/child/children, and a host of other factors. We thought of those things, but didn't get fancy. We simply tried to gauge our sons' reactions and be aware of their needs as they grieved. We knew that even aside from their personality differences, they had obvious dissimilarities and different capacities and abilities to react to death in the family. Debbie could help me with that when Adam died; I had to do it alone the second time around, and frankly, with the distraction of new responsibilities I had to attend to by myself, it was difficult to do it on my own. You may face that challenge.

Common sense teaches that the way we interact with our children and reach their tender hearts is of paramount importance. And while we understand that the developmental differences in our children impact how they each deal with and grow beyond a death in the immediate family, I personally believe there is something larger in the equation, and that is, how *you* deal with it. Stated differently, if you want to improve your children's chances of coping with loss in your family, you must cope well yourself. You lead the way.

My friend Debbie Reeves, who you met earlier, says, "Adversity makes faith real." She is right. The bulwark of strength in times of adversity is not necessarily the one who behaves with an unflinching "life must go on" attitude, who never sheds a tear or communicates sorrow. Instead, the bulwark of strength is the one who frequently prays; who meditates on Scripture and depends deeply on God, for God is the one who delivers us from trouble. The bulwark of strength is the person who relies on the One who is strong—the Rock and Anchor of our souls. Life is ever changing, but God never changes.

Make no mistake; as you try to cope with loss, you may succeed and your children fail; or, you may fail and they may succeed. Hopefully, you'll both succeed. There are no guarantees. But if you want to *improve* your children's chances of getting past loss in their lives, be attentive to their needs; help them as they struggle; answer difficult questions— over and over, if necessary; teach them how to cope with loss with a strong dependence on God; let them watch you and follow your lead. You're the best teacher they have. There's a greater chance they'll grow past tragedy in a healthy way if you grow past it in a healthy way.

Wilson discussed how difficult it is in divorce situations to "get over" the event and experience of loss, and he gave wise suggestions to help. It may not always be the same with death because divorce is not a fact of life. Death is. And with death, you ordinarily *do not* have an adversary who you fear may ignore your children's best interests. That's not always so with divorce.

No doubt, loss for us all is a great misfortune, and it is not easy for us to watch our children learn how difficult life can sometimes be. But whatever the case, if you do your best to cope well yourself, are attentive to your children's needs and behavior, and continue to share with them your reliance (not blame) on God for strength and comfort, they (like the adults around them) can grow from loss. If you need help to help them, to answer their questions, or are concerned about whether they are successfully coping with loss, pray for wisdom, and do not hesitate to reach out to a trusted friend or professional who shares your spiritual values.

Chapter 12

"Dad, She Can't Even Make Kool-Aid®!"

JULIE ADAMS

Why should I have to know how to make Kool-Aid®? At thirty-two years of age and single, there was really no need. I was an R.N. working as a case manager for a home health agency. I wanted to get married, but had not found the right person and had settled in my mind that I was going to stay single.

In the summer of 1990, I learned that a childhood friend was going through a tragedy. His wife had left him and their three children for another man. Even though Wilson and I had known each other since we were kids, nothing had ever been romantic for us. We were like cousins (Wilson's brother is even named after my dad). I had a brief conversation with him one evening and encouraged him to call if he ever needed to talk. A week later, he called and we talked. From then on we talked on a regular basis and from there our relationship changed. We married the next year.

No one knows how he or she will parent until they are one. And the same is true for stepparenting. I certainly had no idea what all was involved in being a stepparent. I had always loved children and had always wanted to be a wife and a mother. Mine just came differently . . . "add a ring and, presto—you're a wife and have three children!" To add even more fun to the "new family," I had been raised an only child without ever encountering the usual sibling rivalries. My world had changed!

I Don't Even Like Roller Coasters

I remember Wilson telling me that marrying him would be like riding a roller coaster. I *thought* I knew what he meant, but years later, I realize I didn't have a clue. Besides, I had forgotten that I don't even like roller coasters! Wilson was still involved with court issues when we married even though he had custody of the children. And in my naiveté, I believed that when a judge evokes rules for families to follow, all would follow. As in many cases, however, the parent without custody *can* and *will* create ways to maneuver around the rules, which only raises the level of frustration.

Suddenly, learning to cook for five while attempting to *please* them all was an impossible task. I expected the kids to like what was prepared and to praise me for being the best cook they had ever known! It wasn't exactly like that. Children believe their mothers to be best because . . . that is all they have ever known. And although we laugh about it now, the day young Dale said, "Dad, she can't even make Kool-Aid®!" was, indeed, a testimony to the fact that I had a lot to learn.

Moving in to another woman's domain was, at the very least, a struggle. Wanting to be conscious of the feelings of the children, it took a long time for me to feel like that home was *my* home. I remember the wallpaper in the den where we spent much of our time—wallpaper that I absolutely detested. After a few months, I began slowly picking at the paper in areas that were not noticeable. It was like therapy . . . gradually allowing me to come in and remove *her* presence. Of course, my presence was a constant reminder to the children that their mother was no longer there.

One night while unloading the dishwasher, I decided that some glasses needed to be thrown away. There was not room for all of them now that *mine* were in the cupboards. I will never forget Dale, who was nine at the time, asking me to please not throw one particular glass away . . . "That's mom's favorite." At the time, I felt a flush of anger with a comment like that, but today it brings tears of sorrow for him.

Being a new wife and mother at the same time also created a few comical moments. A couple of days after we were married, we made a trip to Florida with the children. (Nothing like a honeymoon with three kids!) We stopped at a hotel where the kids enjoyed playing in the pool when a lady sitting nearby asked if they were my children. "Uh . . . yes . . . yes, they are." "How old are they?" she asked. I had the ages memorized and quickly rattled them off. Whew! Then came the curveball I wasn't expecting: "When are their birthdays?" she inquired innocently. Oh no! My mind was at a loss. I couldn't remember. I never looked at the woman's face as she sat waiting for this "mother" to answer a question that should seem so easy. I knew then that the roller coaster of step-parenting would be one wild ride.

Trying to find your place in an already established family is no easy task. But it was important for me (and any woman) to somehow feel settled. Shortly after Wilson and I were married, his ex-wife and her husband moved a few houses down the street from us. Now every time they left *their* house, they drove past *ours*. It felt like all eyes were on me to see how I was functioning and what I was doing. I hated it. Trying to be as stable as possible for the children meant my needs and wants were not the priority. Time eventually took care of the problem as the house was finally sold and we moved to another neighborhood within the same school district.

"Thrilled" was the word describing the feeling of moving into *my* house. The only memories in those walls were the ones *we* would make. The kids were happy and seemed more settled. For the next year, it felt like everyone had a fresh start. We began some of our own family traditions. We added a new dog—a loveable Welsh Corgi/Collie mix we named "Trooper." Months later, however, Wilson's ex-wife moved again . . . one street over from ours. This was not funny anymore. Although it would have been easy to become reclusive in this type of situation, Wilson and I had leaned heavily on one another during a period when we felt like we were being choked. We were in our third year of marriage by now and had already gone through more "stuff" than many have experienced after twenty-five or thirty years of marriage.

I cannot stress enough how important it is to be open and connected with your spouse when trouble arises from the ex-spouse. Wilson and I not only had built a "foundation" on which to live, but also had vowed to stand firm on the foundation of marriage. We were committed to each other, to the children, and foremost, to God.

I learned a lot about prayer in those three years. First of all, I had not done enough of it. And I learned that God does answer. Undoubtedly, I had not been as fervent in my prayer life until I was faced with emotions and situations that were new and frightening. This scripture became my thought for every day—"Do not be anxious about anything, but in everything, by prayer and petition, with thanksgiving, present your requests to God" (Phil. 4:6). In other words, worry about nothing and pray about everything.

Getting the "O" Without the "M"

Making sure the kids were ready for school, fixing breakfast, helping with homework, cooking supper, checking off baths, comforting, refereeing spats, washing clothes, picking up dirty ones, and feeling exhausted at the end of the day was all part of the "O"—as in *occupation*. I had taken on my new occupation, but the title did not come with it . . . as in *Mom*. This part of step-parenting can be the most trying of all. Honestly, I wanted to be called Mom, as I had waited for this part of my life for a very long time. However, it became apparent quickly that the title belonged to someone else . . . someone who wasn't there. A myriad of emotions race through one's mind when there seems to be little recognition of what all had been done and was to come. Wilson did his best to keep me upbeat and told me repeatedly what a great job I was doing. "Not many women would do what you are doing and I love you for it," he would say. But I still longed for that term of endearment from the children.

Crystal was thirty-six months old when I entered her world on a daily basis. My heart ached for her. Her normal childhood had been interrupted forever; her first introduction to adult *selfishness*. She attempted to keep her life as steady as possible and for a while did call me *"Mommy."* She would say it over and over again, as if to convince herself that I was supposed to fit into her puzzle. With time, however, and listening to older siblings call me by my first name, she too reserved that title for someone else.

If you are in a similar situation, then you know the feeling that almost disguises itself as rejection. I have *stepped* in and done the work and filled the empty spot . . . but—only one person can fill the empty spot. As hard and painful as it may be, the spot can only be occupied by the mother or father. And it usually will not matter what *he* or *she* has done. It took me a long time to learn this truth. When I did, it enabled me to relinquish a lot of bitterness.

The pain of abandonment crushes the heart. I cradled all three children at different times while they cried, "Why did she have to go?" "I am so sorry," I would reply. Most of God's created beings are intuitively made to stay close to their young until they are ready to live on their own. Oddly enough, humans can sometimes be the cruelest of all.

I am reminded of the story of a horrific forest fire that raced through the woods causing all of the animals to run as fast as they could. The young were scurrying to stay close to parents for safety. A few days later as forest rangers surveyed the ashes and blackened timber, they stopped in their tracks. Standing stiff and lifeless, covered entirely with black ash, was a bird. It was practically unrecognizable as to its kind. As they gently touched the scorched wings, they heard rustling. Much to their amazement were three young chicks . . . alive. Their mother had protected them with her wings and in so doing had given her own life.

Children scared by divorce will miss the other parent not being in the home as before. Sometimes there is no way to heal the hurt. Over time I have learned that what they "call" me is not what is important. What *is* important is that we learn to love one another, do our best to live right, and remember this was new for everyone. Stepchildren must be allowed to be comfortable with the name they give you. Do not force the issue. Just keep on doing your best to fill that "empty spot." You may be their refuge or, like the bird in the story, you may be their *wings.* Psalm 17:8 says, "Keep me as the apple of the eye, and hide me under the shadow of thy wings."

The Parent Trap

Wilson wrote earlier about the film, *The Parent Trap.* My stepdaughters loved that movie and watched it over and over (and over!) again. On the other hand, I watched it once. The feeling of rejection reared its ugly head when they found such pleasure in this movie, although I am confident that there was no intention of upsetting me. At the time, they did not understand and, at the time, I didn't either. Years later, it has become easier for all of us to talk about it and to get a better picture of how children of divorce handle those situations.

All children attempt to play one parent against another. In the home *without* divorce, children will seek to get mom's approval without consulting dad. When the home is built *because of* divorce, this problem is multiplied. In the above named movie, these twin girls schemed. They planned multiple tricks of deception in order to get their parents back together. And it worked . . . on the Disney set!

As a stepparent, it is very important that you understand that most children want to live with their parents. They want a home with both of them. My youngest stepdaughter cannot remember what it was like to live with both parents. And she, along with her siblings, fell into the *trap* of playing one household against the other, although it took me a while to catch on to what was happening. Because of the continual court battles, it felt like we had to walk on eggs for fear of "anything you say can be used against you in a court of law . . ." So how do you handle it?

I cannot stress enough the importance of the parent and stepparent presenting themselves in the home as *united*. Several years ago, I volunteered for an Internet web site called AllExpert.com in the category of stepparenting (I am no "expert" but do have some real-life experience that should count for something). Interestingly, the most oft-asked questions from stepparent homes was the issue of the "step" parent feeling like the "bio" parent is not handling a situation the way they would, thus creating division in the home. The one thing I tried to help stepparents understand was the guilt that plagues many a custodial parent. They feel sorry for their children having to be split and relocated according to visitation schedules. As a result, discipline often takes a back seat. I mean, how would you like to pack your suitcase each week to meet your scheduled visits? Such a schedule says, "Your time here is temporary." I cringe at some of the visitation schedules for children. One week is here, the next is there, and it goes on and on without end. What a terrible way to experience childhood.

In order to stand united, you will have to pick your battles. Dad or mom will probably make a decision that you know is not in the best interest of the child. If you feel strongly about it, then talk to your spouse. And to those dads and moms . . . please listen to your spouse who is the stepparent. Their opinion may be more objective. There is a temptation to be overly lenient with the kids of divorce. Do not create a crutch for them for, in time, it will not matter to the rest of the world that their parents are divorced.

Deciding discipline in the new household must be a priority. With Wilson's work and being out of town occasionally, it fell to me to discipline the children when he was gone. And they knew that because their father made sure they did. Fortunately, none of them ever said to me, "You are not my mom, I don't have to listen to you." But some kids will say that and the parent must address it. Your job as a stepparent is not to be their friend. As the adult female in the home, I needed to have the authority to enforce the rules. This is not to say that I never had problems deciding what battles to choose. But I had the support of the children's father and it helped our household run more smoothly.

Another factor creating issues is when the two households are on opposite ends regarding discipline. This was true in our case. Rarely would we receive the support we needed to handle certain situations. This not only caused tension between households, it sent the wrong message to the kids and created an environment of disobedience. Communication is the key when addressing this matter. If at all possible, get on the same page with discipline. The children will feel more secure and be less likely to create havoc for all parents.

There will be days when you will wonder if the battles you are fighting will win the war. And even though those children are not yours physically, it is still your responsibility to be an example to them that reflects the will of God in *your* life. Remember this verse: "I can do all things through Christ who strengthens me" (Phil. 4:13).

The Rude Awakening

It was a January morning in 2001 and I had worked the night shift at the hospital. I got home before the kids went to school, wished them a good day, talked to Wilson briefly before he went to work, and headed to bed. Around midmorning the dogs started barking and I awoke to see a sheriff's car in our driveway. Not usually good news. My heart sank as I quickly put on a robe and answered the door. "Does Wilson Adams live here?" he asked. "Yes, he does," I replied. "I have some court papers for him and need his signature," he continued. I let the sheriff know that Wilson was at work and that we would drive to the courthouse to receive them. Before he left, I glanced at the papers. I immediately recognized *her* name. My heart began racing. Somehow, it always seemed that when things were going better than before, the *roller coaster* would take another *dive*.

We went to the courthouse where we sat and read together. Our hearts were breaking as we realized that once again, we were headed to battle. This time, however, it was different. Not only was there a request for change of custody for our now thirteen-year-old daughter, but also there were accusations of child abuse against us. The horror of reading that you are a child abuser is almost unbearable. We both knew neither of us had done these things but would now be forced to defend ourselves.

I did not know how much more of this I could take. The thought of being accused of such a horrible crime tore me up inside. I had gone from sobbing to writhing in anguish. And to this day it is emotional for me. We were five months away from the planned wedding of our oldest stepdaughter that, at her request, was going to be in our side yard. We were also in the middle of planting a new church. My cup was running over.

With much prayer and belief that the Lord would see us through, we pulled ourselves together and began the battle. As a registered nurse, it was important that my name be cleared. We called child protective services and asked if there had been anything filed. They said no. I described our situation and asked them to come to our home for a case study if needed. It wasn't. I also sought counsel from a nurse attorney who gave advice should I need it.

Together we researched child abuse allegations. In divorce cases, many experts estimate that approximately 80 percent of reports of child abuse are false. Studies have shown that many non-custodial parents will deliberately make false allegations seeking to regain custody. The report also found that those wrongfully charged with child abuse suffer more than those wrongfully accused of other crimes.

For over two years, Wilson and I had this dark cloud hanging over our heads. It took that long for it to be settled. In those two years, I released the anger and bitterness that had taken over my heart and called on God to let this cup pass from me. Aloud I prayed for healing to my broken heart and to deliver me from Satan who had invaded our home. The Father answered my prayer and I was loosed from the grip of the evil one.

No reports were ever filed, the allegations were false, and our names were cleared. We became part of that 80 percent statistic.

It is difficult to know how to work with parents who do not follow rules, whether God's or the government's. I ran the gamut of emotions and will be the first to say that I did not always choose the right and best way to handle a situation. If conversations and decisions can be made without animosity, someone will have to acquiesce. Naturally, the best-case scenario would be that the custodial parent always makes decisions and does the communicating. But that is not always possible.

You Can Do This!

My stepchildren have seen me struggle with issues where their mother was involved. As they pass through different stages in their own lives, I am still learning how best to react. It was always my prayer and motive for them to remain strong in their faith. My tongue has hurt them (unintentionally) and also healed them. You don't always know the right thing to say and hindsight would be wonderful for us all. But Wilson, the children, and I have bonded in an unusual way. This bond stems foremost from wanting to do right in the sight of God and from that commitment we have *learned* to love one another. We now have a granddaughter who is our absolute delight. She calls us *her Nana* and *her Beba*. I like that.

Stepping into your parent role does not automatically evoke love from your stepchildren. You have to earn it. I wish they had known me before I put on my "fatigues." Because of my love for my husband, I willingly submitted to the battle. We have worked hard to learn Who is ultimately in control and most of all . . . I have learned about myself.

May this verse help those who walk in the most challenging of callings—"the stepparent"—

> No temptation has seized you except what is common to man. And God is faithful; he will not let you be tempted beyond what you can bear. But when you are tempted, he will also provide a way out so that you can stand up under it.
> —1 Corinthians 10:13

Chapter 13

Blue Skies and
Rainbows

DEBBIE (REEVES) LANPHEAR

Even though you've read this far, you may still ask yourself, "Will I ever feel better or be happy again after what I've been through? My life is shattered and can never be the same." Of course, it *won't* ever be the same, but it can be wonderful again. This is *not* just an empty platitude. God is able to make blue skies and rainbows out of the dark clouds you're in right now. There is hope. I know, because I have been through those dark clouds myself.

Wilson previously wrote that everyone has a story. It's true. The Bible tells us about countless people, such as the Shunamite woman (2 Kings 4:8–37), the widow of Nain (Luke 7:11–17), and the woman who met Jesus at the well (John 4:7–28)—all women who remain nameless in Scripture but who are not nameless to God. The Great Creator of this world knew their names, their hurts, and their sufferings, and He knows ours as well. Jesus said that God is aware of each tiny sparrow. "Do not fear therefore;" He says, "you are of more value than many sparrows" (Matt. 10:29–31 NKJV). He watches over all of us, including you, too. How do I know? Let me share some of my own story . . .

My life, like yours, hasn't always been picture perfect. I hoped as a young girl that my prince on his white horse would whisk me off to his cottage, with its flower-laced picket fence, and we'd live happily ever after. Truthfully, as an adult I realized that that vision of life isn't reality, and I really didn't expect Prince Charming, the little white house, or the picket fence, but my perspective was that if I obeyed God and followed His truth, I would have a happy life. My parents, Ann and Hubert, had been happily married for almost twenty-five years, and had created a wonderful family environment for me and my brothers and sister, so my expectations were understandably high. I didn't aspire for a career, a huge home, or wealth; I simply wanted to marry a man who loved God and me, and to have a family. I knew that "happily ever after" would have a few bumps, since that's life, but figured that everything would pretty much work out.

I graduated from high school in 1972, set off to college, and met "the man of my dreams." The next year, we married. Within a few years, he began to preach at the small church where we worshipped, and we settled down to life as I expected it—only it wasn't what I expected at all. Almost from the beginning, he exhibited a Jekyll and Hyde personality, with radical mood swings and unexplained rages. Early on, I felt I was able to help pull him out of the dark moods, but as time passed, I realized I couldn't. It was frighteningly unpredictable behavior, and his episodes gradually increased in frequency and intensity. He often locked me out of our bedroom if I said or did anything that displeased him. We lived on a farm in rural Alabama near Birmingham, and late one night he got so angry with me that he drug me from the bathtub onto the front porch, and locked me outside our home. He wouldn't let me back in until I said what he wanted to hear. But that was only one of many similar incidents.

I loved the good and kind man he could be, and hated the scary, violent stranger that seemed to take hold of him more and more often. I cannot count the number of times he knocked my glasses off my face, drug me by the hair, or shook me like a rag doll. I constantly hid the bruises on my arms and legs. As his behavior became increasingly abusive, he began to behave inappropriately with a twenty-two-year-old woman we had befriended. When I confronted him about her, he clamped his hand over my nose and mouth so that I couldn't breathe. I truly thought I was going to die—and that happened more than once. Despite my protests, he openly flaunted their relationship with weekly horseback rides and ice skate nights.

As he spent more time with her, his behavior at home worsened. He began to withdraw, and seclude himself in our basement. He had virtually no relationship with our sons or with me. Our marriage was in extraordinary crisis. He wanted me to run, but I refused. I was committed to persevere because I'd committed to God to do it. I prayed daily that God would intervene, and save our family. I was in the fight of my life . . . I wish I could tell you that everything worked out, but in April 1993, after nearly twenty years of a difficult, heartbreaking marriage, our lives took a disastrous turn.

Reality

On the Saturday before my thirty-ninth birthday, our family had been invited to celebrate at my twin brother David's home a couple of hours away. Although Michael, our eighteen-year-old son, was away at college, I expected that we—including our two other sons, Gabriel and Nathanael, aged fifteen and ten—would spend the day at my brother's with us. When I awoke, my husband was already up, dressed, and about to leave the house. He didn't tell me where he was going—his habit for the past several months. I could feel the tension in our relationship, and knew our marriage was disintegrating. I reminded him of our birthday plans, but he coldly said he had no interest in any birthday party, and left the house. I wiped my tears away. I didn't want the boys to see me cry—again. The boys and I got ready to go, and went to the party with my mom and dad. I tried to put our difficulties out of mind and have a fun day.

At 11:00 P.M. the boys and I returned home. As we walked in the door, a large moving box sat askew in the entryway. A coat hanger and necktie hung on it at an odd angle as if someone had left hurriedly. Our home office had been emptied of the computer, books, television—everything. It looked like we'd been burglarized. In my heart of hearts I knew what had happened, but momentarily refused to believe it. I ran up the stairs, two at a time, to see if my husband's clothes were in his closet. It was empty. So was his chest of drawers. The unthinkable had happened; he left us for her.

For months, I'd fought battle after battle for my marriage-in-crisis, and now feared I'd lost the war. I was gripped in shock; I couldn't believe it had happened. I felt like the wind had been knocked out of me. The boys followed me through the house in stunned silence. I checked the answering machine to see if he'd left a message. A curt voicemail said: "I've left your mother, but haven't left you. I can't tell you where I've gone, but I'll get in touch with you later."

I didn't know what to do. Overcome with panic, my hands shook while I dialed the phone for my parents who, only minutes before, had dropped us off. Oh, how much life had changed in those few minutes! I sobbed as I explained what had happened. Like me, they were in disbelief. They reassured me that everything would be all right and offered to come and get us. Although they calmed me, I felt like the boys and I had been cut adrift from a sinking ship in the dead of night with no supplies. I was absolutely shattered. I hurt for my sons and for me. Where were we supposed to go from here?

A few days before, I'd confided to my brother Dan that my husband's behavior was worse than ever, and relayed my concern for what might happen. He was already aware of our situation, and told me that I needed to find a job because "the wheels might come off the wagon." I replied that since I had not finished college, but had been a stay-at-home-cookie-baking-preacher's-wife for almost twenty years, that didn't exactly qualify me for much in the business world.

"You better find a job," he said matter-of-factly.

Without much confidence, I marked several Help Wanted ads from the newspaper, and asked my aunt, a business owner, for advice about what to do. I told her I'd seen an opening for a layout artist at a large print company nearby. She told me, "Call them up and tell them you'll work six weeks for nothing, and ask if they've had a better offer today!" I wrote down everything she said, hung up the phone, and quickly dialed the number before I could chicken out.

The department head, a kind man named Dominic, answered the phone and I told him I'd work six weeks for nothing.

Surprised, he said, "You're serious, aren't you?"

"Yes, I am," I said. "I need a job."

"Come in tomorrow for an interview, and bring your portfolio."

That was on Thursday, two days before my husband disappeared.

Astonished, I thanked Dominic and arranged an appointment for the next day. The problem was I didn't have a portfolio, and I'd never had a professional job interview. That evening, I called a friend who was in graphic arts school. She told me how to prepare a portfolio, and encouraged me with these words: "Drink a pot of coffee and charge in and sell yourself!" Although I didn't feel like I had much to sell, I stayed up to the wee hours of the morning to finish the "portfolio" while my husband was isolated in the basement. The next day, I summoned the courage to get up and go, and prayed as I drove that God would help me get the job.

During the interview, Dominic turned his chair away from me to take a phone call. I looked at a stack of résumés an inch-and-a-half thick lying on his desk. *What am I doing here?* I thought to myself. *I don't have a chance.* It was an "O ye of little faith" moment. Though I didn't realize it at the time, I put forth the effort, and God took care of the rest.

The following Monday—after the cataclysmic events of Saturday— Dominic called me to explain that the job was between me and two other women. We were to compete against each other for three days, and he would award the job to one of us afterward. On the fourth day, he eliminated one applicant, and the other decided she didn't want the position. "Congratulations," he told me at the end of the week. "The job is yours."

I could hardly believe my ears! It was the small wonder I needed to raise my hopes. My husband left us on Saturday, and I had a job on Monday! It was God's reminder that He would provide for us.

My husband began to make disturbing threats and phone calls to me. He carried a gun around town, and friends reported sightings to me of him and his girlfriend. He ignored court orders and repeatedly showed up at our home to carry off whatever he wanted by the trailer load. It made no difference if the doors were locked, and it seemed there was nothing we could do to stop him. He even took the family dog, our sons' computer, and the box of family photos. I knew that if we stayed we would have nothing left. We simply wanted him to leave us alone.

Child support was sporadic and unreliable, and I couldn't afford the mortgage payments, so we moved in temporarily with my parents. A couple months later, they generously helped us purchase a mobile home, and we tried to start a new life. I felt like my life was over, but God knew differently. Had I looked closer, I would have seen how compassionate He was. Family and friends provided for us over and over. I don't know how we would have gotten by otherwise.

Nonetheless, it was a dreary time and I was angry. I felt like my sons and I were robbed of the life we were supposed to have, not the one we actually lived. I was so blinded by what I thought I'd lost that I couldn't see what I still had. I spent too much time grieving for what I expected and too little time thankful for my blessings. I thought it was the most difficult of times, but didn't know the worst was yet to come.

We tried to put life back together again, but it is hard as a single parent. The grind of my job and strain of responsibilities at home was tiring, and I was struggling to recover emotionally. I left for work each morning before the boys left for school, and when I got home, I was so busy with "mom" duties that it was hard to be a . . . *Mom.* On January 31, 1994, I specifically recall telling a co-worker at the end of the day, "Now I have to go home to my second job." How I wish I had never said that. If only I'd known.

The Day

The next day was a cold Tuesday morning. The boys were still in their beds as I prepared to leave. I told them I loved them and kissed them goodbye. Gabriel's eyelids fluttered, but he didn't wake. I hurried out the door. About an hour later, one of my co-workers came to the desk where I stood, put her arms on each side of me and quietly said, "Your boys have been in an accident." It strangely felt like an out-of-body experience. I remember thinking, "Okay, you knew someday something like this could happen, so how are you going to deal with it?" I said nothing, but shook as I gathered my things. Three members of my office volunteered to drive me to the hospital, and accompanied me out of the shop. It was a large building, and as I walked to the door, people began to gather with sad looks on their faces. When I got to the back door, I turned to Peggy, one of my co-workers, to ask if my boys were all right. She said, "Debbie, please don't ask me any more questions." At that moment, I realized that one or both of my boys could be gone and I began to cry.

The ride to Birmingham's Children's Hospital was the longest ride of my life. I cried and prayed the whole time, remembering my prayer each morning on the way to work that my boys would be safe on their drive to school. When we reached the hospital, my parents, brother, and our friend, Sheriff Jones were there. As I hurried to them, my brother Dan gathered me in his arms. I hoped against hope that he would tell me they were okay, but as I looked into his eyes, he whispered, "Deb, Gabriel did not make it."

I fell onto his shoulder and cried, "Not my Gabriel! Not my precious Gabriel!"

I couldn't believe this was happening. None of it seemed real. I wanted to wake up and find it was a very bad dream, and that everything was right in the world. But it wasn't. I later learned that when Gabriel and Nathanael were almost to school, Gabriel crossed the yellow line a mere fifteen inches, and met an oncoming car. They collided. Gabriel died instantly.

Doctors told me that they weren't yet certain of the extent of Nathanael's injuries, but that I could see him. He was still in a state of shock, unaware that his brother had died, and he looked so small and helpless and in such pain. My heart ached for him. I wanted to make it all better, but I couldn't. He had a broken leg and numerous injuries to his face and neck, but I was so thankful he was alive. Family and Christian friends began to gather at the hospital to surround us with their love.

Michael and his fiancée immediately drove with a group of their friends from the college in Florida where he attended and we all sat that night in vigil near Nathanael's room. Sometime during the night, they took a walk and I was finally alone with my thoughts for the very first time. I remember feeling such pain that I couldn't lay still. It was as if I could feel God's presence beside me, with His hand on my shoulder to help me. I thought I'd known grief before now, but I hurt in a completely different way, and truly began to understand Isaiah's description of the Lord as a man of sorrows, acquainted with grief (Isa. 53:3).

Nathanael's doctors released him from the hospital to attend the funeral. Our friends and Christian family comforted us, but nothing could really take away the pain. I wondered how we could ever recover from this.

The collision broke Nathanael's tibia completely in two, and he wore a large cast from his hip to the end of his foot. Staples sutured several injuries on his face. Doctors also discovered a small piece of glass in his brow that had to be surgically removed. His leg took six long months to heal, and he required special care the entire time. I was just thankful that he was alive, but I was as concerned about the condition of his broken heart as much as anything else.

Survival

The boys had now lost their dad and their brother. Our family of five was now down to three, and all of us were wounded on so many levels. I wanted to circle our wagons because I felt like our family was vulnerable to another attack. We were in survival mode. The next few years would be challenging.

People ask me how I did it. We clung to each other and to God. It was either "get up" or "give up." I never thought I had a choice. Death had come to visit, and I had to decide if I was going to deal with it and move forward, or let it become a macabre fixture in our lives. Grief work is hard and it taught me so very much about God's love and about myself.

One of the lessons I learned is that no matter how difficult and dark things are, there are always blessings to count. I did not do that after my husband left. I was angry that my life and the lives of my boys had been shattered. I had always been able to be at home and did not like being in the work world. I felt like a square peg in a round hole. I was so foolish that Monday night before Gabriel's accident when I told one of my co-workers I was going home to my second job. If only I'd realized it was my last night to spend with my precious Gabriel, how different my attitude would have been. I would give *anything* now to have that evening to spend over again. I would make the most of every minute. What a hard way to learn perspective. I have promised myself that I will never say such a thing again. Life can change on a dime, and in a moment, everything I have can be gone, including my loved ones. When that lesson comes home to you, you begin to count the moments with all the people you love.

I also realized that God was truly my sanctuary in everything, great or small. Isaiah 66:13 says, "As a mother comforts her child, so will I comfort you." I went to Him with *all* of my problems—literally! It seems funny now, but at one point I was driving a car that I later sold at a yard sale for $700. When the air conditioner went out during the hottest part of the Alabama summer, I stopped at a small auto repair shop on my way to work where my friend, Davy, specialized in air-conditioning repair. He said it was probably going to be the air conditioner clutch, and it would cost $75 to fix it. He asked me to call him later that morning so he could give me the verdict. To me that was a fortune, and I didn't have $75. Truthfully, I didn't have two nickels to rub together, so I said a prayer that I could afford to get it fixed. Later, I called him, and he said he had good news and bad news.

"Well, give me the bad news first," I said.

He replied, "It's the clutch."

I wailed, "Then how can there be any good news?"

Davy laughed and said, "Ms. Debbie, I've been fixin' air conditioners for years and I've never seen this happen before, but every piece of that clutch had fallen out under your car and was caught, and I was able to put it together and it's working. It'll cost you $21.00."

Our driveway was a very bumpy dirt road, which made it all the more improbable, but I am convinced that it was the unexplained, providential care of the Lord that happened so often. There were countless other times when I was at my lowest and I would get a card or a phone call full of spiritual encouragement—always when I needed it.

I talked with God every chance I got, and learned that it was He who now cared for my sons, for Gabriel, and for me. Gabriel was now in the safe refuge of His arms. "God is our refuge and strength, a very present help in trouble" (Ps. 46:1 KJV), and I was so small; who was I that He would care so much for me (Ps. 8:4)? I knew that without God I was nothing, and that He carried me like a child.

Decisions

We began the tough task of making sense of our lives. I worked at the printing company for another year, and was then offered a job by an insurance agent in the small town near our farm. I eagerly took it to be closer to Nathanael, and worked there for two years. Meanwhile, Michael finished college and married in 1995, and they moved to Kentucky to go to school. I eventually took a position at an elementary school as a teacher's aide for special needs children. I loved my work— it brought me joy and lacked the stress of my previous jobs—but after two years there, we were struggling financially. I hadn't received child support for several years, and my ex-husband was in hiding out-of-state. It was difficult to make ends meet.

I wanted to go back to college to complete my degree so I could increase my earning power, but I was concerned about college consuming too much of my time and attention. Nathanael was now in high school and I felt that he needed me now more than ever. I prayed for direction and applied to the University of Montevallo. My application was approved and financial aid was arranged! I purchased a parking pass and went to orientation, eagerly awaiting classes to begin after the new year. One thing I didn't know was that God was about to take my life on another unexpected turn . . .

It was a quiet morning in January 1999 and I was enjoying the last of the holiday before school started, when the phone rang in the other room. I hurried to pick it up and Sheriff Jones was on the line. He and his wife were longtime friends and had seen us through our many difficulties the previous years. He started, "Debbie (his wife) and I have been talking, and I was just led to call you. We are looking for a director for the county work release program, and I've submitted your name. Are you interested?" He paused to let it sink in. "I know you love your job working with the children, but if you want to help people, this is the job for you."

I couldn't believe what I'd heard. I had to squelch the urge to hold the phone away from my ear and look at it to make sure he was talking to me. "Yes, helping people is what I want to do," I said.

He continued, "Well, you know you will be helping the children even more if you can help their parents. I believe it would be a job that is a perfect fit for you. I've prayed about this . . ."

"I'll pray about it, too," I said. "If the Lord wants me to do this, He'll open a door." Again, I had an "O ye of little faith" moment as I thought, *I won't get this job,* but I heard myself say, "Sure, I'll apply."

He went on to explain a little more about his vision for the program and we set up the interview. Two weeks later, just before school was to start, I received the call that I got the job! Here I was at a crossroads, and the Lord pointed in a totally different direction than I had planned. But I had asked for His direction and had gotten my answer.

I must say that I was terrified when I had to represent the program for the first time in court, but I purchased a red suit, found a briefcase, and said a prayer. I reminded myself often that God helped Moses when he went before Pharaoh, and He would help me, too. I laughed when my sister-in-law, Jan, came to work with me. I told her that like Moses, I had asked God for a helper and He had sent him Aaron, and that she was to be my Aaron.

With God's guidance, I went from being a stay-at-home mom in 1993 to overseeing a Work Release Program in 1999. What a journey He had taken me on in my work life. One of the hurtful things that my husband had flung at me when he had left so long ago was that I wouldn't last a day in the business world. God was trying to teach me, though, that He and I could make it together. When I was hired, the program was a monthly reporting probation program with weekend community service for nonviolent felons and misdemeanors cases. Within two-and-a-half years, it grew to a Community Corrections program—a 100-bed residential center for men and women, complete with a comprehensive drug testing program and all the related services. And I was the Director.

"Toto, we're not in Kansas anymore . . ."

On the home front, Nathanael and I had been lonely those first few years, but God brought someone special into our lives. He was a Sheriff's Deputy named Bubba, a wonderful man. We dated for a while and he became a Christian. He filled a needed role of company, friendship, and safety to both Nathanael and me, but as time passed, I hesitated to continue a relationship that did not seem to move forward. For a long time I had prayed to the Lord for someone to marry, but it seemed it was not to be. Heartbroken, we agreed to remain as friends. I had moved into a new home on the farm my parents owned and life was moving on. I could look back over the last few years and see that God had carried me through my heartaches and trials, and I had been richly blessed.

It was late 2004, and most all of my family lived around me on the farm. My son, Michael, and his wife, Pippa, and my two grandsons, Gabriel and Titus—yes, Gabriel's namesakes—had moved in 2002 from Bowling Green, Kentucky, to build a house next door to me. Nathanael was serving as a Black Hawk helicopter crew chief with the 160th Airborne Division, and he and his wife, Katy, were healthy, doing well and prospering spiritually. My parents lived on the farm. My brothers, Dan and David, and sister, Beth, and their families all lived around me on their land, and I had a wonderful job working with Community Corrections. The direction of my life seemed set.

Peace

When I came home from work that night in December, I stopped by my parents' home for a short visit. I was finally at peace with the idea that this was to be my life and I would spend it alone. I told my mom that night, "Well, I'm not expecting to ever find anyone with whom to share my life. I am too old to be looking or expecting it and I'm not going to pray for it anymore. God has said He will provide *all* that I need, so if He wants me to have a relationship, He'll either drop it in my lap or it will run me down, because I am content with my life. Anyway," I said with a grin, "Prince Charming is dead now, if he ever existed." I drove home that night and slept well. I had finally accepted that God was keeping watch over me.

It had taken me eleven long years to get to the point where I was at peace with what my life would be like. I *thought* I was at peace years before, but didn't realize that I hadn't as yet laid everything at His feet and that I was still holding onto my expectations. I finally came to understand that if He gave his Son to save me, He would also provide everything else that I needed as He promised. He didn't need my help. He could do far more wonderful things with my life than I could. He could bring me to and through things that I never would have imagined. I now began to appreciate what it is to be content and I felt so very blessed. God promises, "Those who sow in tears will reap with songs of joy" (Ps. 126:5). Part of that joy is being content with what you have, with the confidence that God is giving you all you need for the time.

Scripture tells us in Jeremiah 29:11, "I know the plans I have for you . . . plans to give you hope and a future." That is God's declaration to those who obey Him. It is so difficult to grasp that truth when you're in the middle of trials and tragedies, but I can look back now and see how He gathered my shattered shell of a life, and held my spirit together in the palm of His strong hands.

God brought me through the awful storms and dark clouds to blue skies and rainbows . . .

. . . and I can't wait for tomorrow.

Epilogue

DAVID

A lone at fifty."
I looked at my friend with a blank, empty stare, and said it again.
"I'm alone at fifty."

The words just fell from my mouth, in disbelief, with hardly a breath. How could this be? Debbie lay in the Critical Care Unit in the room next door, her condition growing dimmer each day, and my future suddenly seemed so different—so grim, gray, and lonely. Was it a selfish moment? I hope not. I was simply grasping for the first time since the whirlwind events of that horrible week had started that at the end I would likely be alone. Alone—for the first time in thirty-plus years. Alone—without my best friend, my children's mother, my college sweetheart, and the smile I came home to each evening.

Technically, I wasn't alone. I was surrounded by my sons, our family, and many, many friends and fellow Christians, who loved us and cared for us, and did everything they could to help us. And I was busy with all the things I had to do, not only then, but in the weeks and months that followed. But I missed *her*! A sea of people surrounded me, but I missed *her*! I felt like I was in a vast, dry emotional wasteland, all by myself. I was alone!

I'm still young, in good health, with lots of productive years ahead of me. There are lots of things I want to do. This is the fall, not winter, of my life, and I don't want to be alone!

Alone. It's such a painful word.

But my story doesn't stop there. Time doesn't stop in the middle of grief and sorrow. It may *seem* that way because you travel in it for so long, but it doesn't stop. It didn't stop for me, and it won't stop for you. It was hard for me to grasp that in the middle of the pain, and it may be hard for you. But keep hanging on. You're moving, and at some moment in time in the dark shadows of this deep, deep valley, the light will begin to creep back into life. Trust me. I've been through this valley before.

The Presence of Absence

After Debbie died, I went on automatic pilot and tried to learn how to do all the things she did for our family, and at the same time, continue to do the things I did. Frankly, it was impossible. It was an unpleasant, unfamiliar role—trying to balance career and household duties, and do it all myself. I started early in the morning and finished late at night, and every day, I felt it—I was alone. I felt alone in the morning getting ready for work; in the evening when I returned home; every night when I went to bed. I felt alone in the grocery learning to shop and at a restaurant table for two. Everywhere it should have been "us" it was just "me." My friend, L.A. Stauffer, calls it "the presence of absence."

Consequently, I prayed. *Every day* I prayed that if it was God's will that I should marry again that He give me a godly, Christian woman who would help me get to heaven. I described this woman to God in my prayers, and told Him in detail the kind of marriage and marriage partner I wanted to have—someone who would love Him, love me, and my children. And I asked Him to lift the awful weight of heartache and loneliness from me, and to use me in His service and His glory. But in all things, I wanted God's will for me. I gave it to God.

And all the while, I battled with grief and loss for my sweet wife, and struggled with old wounds from Adam's death, and the darkness in the shadow of the valley just engulfed me.

But that's not the end of my story. Time didn't stop there.

Wilson and I had been friends for several years, and during the fall before Debbie's death, we had traveled together with a group of other guys to hike Montana's Glacier National Park. During that trip, in the midst of the awesome beauty of God's creation, I had shared with my friends the awful struggle of losing a child and the difficult road to recovery. Now, nine months later, I was mired again in the anguish of grief over Debbie.

Wilson and Julie lived only forty-five minutes away—I was in Bowling Green, Kentucky and they were near Nashville—and we kept in close contact. Wilson and I exchanged e-mails almost daily, and shared our hearts about loss and how we'd coped, and the similarities and dissimilarities of our losses. And from those discussions, in the fall of 2004 grew the idea for this book.

Coincidence or Providence?

As we planned our book project, we wanted to speak with others who had shared similar experiences, and learn how they survived. One night in December, Wilson shared with me an e-mail he had received from his longtime friend, Colly Caldwell, the president of Florida College in Tampa. Wilson had contacted Colly to tell him about our project and ask if he knew anyone we could interview. Colly's e-mail identified an acquaintance in Alabama, a woman named Debbie Reeves, who had endured divorce and then the loss of her son, all in less than a year.

A few weeks later, Julie contacted Debbie, told her about our project, and invited her to their home for a weekend of sharing. She consented. So it was that Friday night in late January 2005 that I met her. We learned that we had so many things in common: she, like me, was a twin, and her twin brother's name was David; we both had three sons and had both lost one in auto accidents; her Gabriel's birthday was on November 22, the same date as my Debbie; she, like Debbie, had come from a family of two boys and two girls; and as odd as it might be, her name was Debbie, too.

I also learned that her son, Michael, and his family had lived in Bowling Green for six years, and even though I didn't know them, my son Colin did. In fact, we realized, Michael had lived in a subdivision directly across the road from our home for several years before they returned to Alabama in 2001, and we shared some of the same friends and acquaintances. Although she had visited Michael in Bowling Green dozens of times through the years, like ships in the night, *our* paths had never crossed.

In time, we realized even more. When Adam died in 1999, and we were struggling so with his death, one of my Debbie's close friends had visited our home to tell her about a friend of hers in Alabama who had lost a son in an auto accident. "I talked with her," she said, "and she would be glad to talk with you if you want," Debbie's friend explained. "Here's her number, if you like."

After she left, I asked Debbie if she was going to call the lady from Alabama. "Not right now. I don't want to talk to someone else, yet," she said. She never called. That number, I since learned, belonged to . . . *Debbie Reeves.*

And that's not all, but it's enough for now.

As Debbie Reeves explained earlier, less than a week after she told her mother in December 2004 that she was finally at peace with her life, and that God would provide everything she needed—even companionship if that was what she should have—Colly Caldwell called her to ask if she would share her story with us.

We first met in January, but it was not our last meeting. We continued to share and get together, even long distance, though both of us were cautious not to make more of our acquaintance than we should. I continued to pray for guidance, and must tell you that she was (and is), in the flesh, the woman of my prayers. Love flourished again, and we married on July 16 of that year. God has blessed us so richly. We are happy! We can smile! We look forward to the future!

My friends, Wilson and Julie, in Tennessee, who knew me but not her, contacted their friend, Colly, in Florida, who knew her but not me, who contacted her in Alabama, and asked if she would help this man from Kentucky. Convoluted coincidence? We will always believe in the power of God's providence.

The great irony is that had we each not lost our sons and our spouses, had we not traveled through the tortuous journey of grief and loss, we would have never met or shared the joy we now share. That doesn't mean that we are happy we went through our losses, but it does mean that God provides, in His time, and when we trust Him, He *will* deliver us from tragedy and misfortune (Rom. 8:28).

Life can throw you a curve. You know that. And the road you now travel is difficult. I know that. The challenges Wilson and I have written about have you in an awful place, and it is a dreary time. But be patient! Hope and healing are on the way! I am witness to it! The path to the Cure is well traveled, and He provides peace and solace like no other. Trust Him! Seek Him! Find Him! Your life—and *you*—will never be the same.

<hr />

WILSON

I was fortunate to share lunch and an afternoon recently with leadership guru John Maxwell. Maxwell knows his stuff. One of his favorite sayings is that "defining moments define us." He says, "Defining moments put the spotlight on us . . . our character isn't made during these times—it is displayed!"

Defining moments . . . As I thought about John's words, two truths about defining moments became evident: 1) we all have them; and, 2) you will never be the same afterward. In this book, we have invited you to share some very personal and private *defining moments* with us. In all probability you saw yourself somewhere within these pages. And why? Because we all suffer and hurt; each of us face defining moments. While our stories are all too real to us, we recognize that your story is just as real to you. The question, then, is not will defining moments come into all of our lives (they will); the question is—will I have the faith and fortitude to show family and friends that I trust in God's providential care even when I do not understand?

Regardless of the defining moment, you will never be the same. Somehow you will be moved. You may move backward or forward, but you will be moved. Defining moments are not normal. They knock you into abnormality, leaving you battered against the ropes. They leave you with the same sick feeling you experienced when you fell on the playground as a youngster and had the wind knocked out of your lungs. You wondered for a moment if you would ever breathe and live again. Although shaken and scared, you survived.

And you will survive now, but you will be different.

I think of the three Hebrew boys, Shadrach, Meshach, and Abednego whose story is told in Daniel 3. Those young men stood their ground against the evil Nebuchadnezzar who ordered them and everyone else to worship before his image of gold. As a result of their refusal, they were cast into a furnace of fire. But remember their words to the Babylonian dictator just prior to what everyone thought would be their death? Daniel 3:17–18—

> If it be so, our God whom we serve is able to deliver us from the furnace of blazing fire; and He will deliver us out of your hand O king. But even if He does not, let it be known to you . . . that we are not going to serve your gods or worship the golden image that you have set up.
>
> —Daniel 3:17–18

I would say that was a defining moment. The moment was defined further when they later appeared unharmed. None of us were there, but I can only say from human experience that the three boys who came out the other side of the fire of testing were not the same. And never would be. Defining moments change us. It changed them for the better.

Or take Peter. The night of his three-fold denials was a defining moment. Such a scar would destroy most of us. But by the grace of God, Peter was able to translate failure into progress. One moment he is left alone in a darkened corner heaving sobs of heavy regret; and days later he is preaching for all of his life (literally!) to the some of the same ones who had demanded that Jesus be crucified. Peter had turned a defining moment into an opportunity for God's grace to shine.

And so can you.

Faith Matters

God cannot use you greatly until He has broken you completely. Perhaps you are currently in the cave of your defining moment. You see no way out; no end in sight; and no way God can use this for His glory. Don't be so sure. "'For I know the plans I have for you,' declares the Lord, 'plans for welfare and not for calamity to give you a future and a hope. Then you will call upon Me and come and pray to me, and I will answer'" (Jer. 29:11–12). Although it was a prophetic message to the remnant of God's people in the Old Testament, the principle remains in effect still today (Rom. 8:28).

Author Philip Yancey says, "Faith is trusting in advance what will only make sense in reverse." Every parent understands. Small children ask tons of questions and most of the time we can satisfy their curiosity with simple answers. But the day will come when they will need answers of more substance—answers that may not square with their lack of life experience. And that's when we have to say, "Trust me."

God may be saying that to you right now.

These defining moments are not disturbing interruptions on the path of our progress—they *are* the path to our progress. Through them God molds our hearts and shapes us into the kind of men and women He wants us to be. Your faith will help you through a crisis for sure, but more than that, your faith will enable you to come forth with a whole new perspective about life. You will not be the same. Ever. You will be better.

And that is your choice: to become *bitter* or *better*. It is a choice that all of us make. I cannot choose my circumstances, but I can choose my response and attitude toward them. Sadly, I have known several who marched to the beat of self-pity, drew the shades, and sang the woe-is-me refrain to as many as would listen (crowds tend to become smaller as time progresses). On the other hand, I have known those who have faced the worst of human tragedy only to emerge as shining examples of the strength that only God provides. Those people inspire me.

A Time for Every Season

Solomon reminds us that God can make all things beautiful in its time (Eccl. 3:11a)—but only if you will let Him. The power of His creativity in the world is nothing compared to what He can create from a broken and shattered life. He can pick up pieces. He can put you back together. Granted, you may not be the same person you were, but by God's strength, you will be *better!*

I conclude by asking you three questions. I only ask for an honest and thorough soul-searching as you ponder your answers. Here goes:

1. *What is your unjust disadvantage?* You have one. We all do. What is the cause of your struggle; the thing that robs you of sleep and peace? Ill health? A hurting marriage? Prodigal children? Job loss? Financial reversal? Divorce? Single parenthood? Stepparenthood? Cancer? Hard and hurt feelings with in-laws? A haunting sin in the closet of your past? The death of a child? The death of a spouse? Caregiving 24/7 for aging parents? The ache of loneliness? The memory of abuse? What is *your* unjust disadvantage?

2. *When do you plan to replace self-pity with faith-filled courage?* Just when do you plan on stopping the "woe-is-me" whine and start thinking: "Wait a minute! I have a distinct message to the world . . ."

One of my favorite books is *The Ultimate Gift* by Tom Sullivan. Sullivan is a world-class athlete with two national championships in wrestling. He was on the 1958 Olympic team. He earned a degree at Harvard in clinical psychology. He is a musician. He is a sports enthusiast. He swims and skydives. Last year, Tom's book became a movie by the same name (if you haven't seen it—see it).

I should also tell you one more thing—Tom Sullivan is blind.

In his talks around the country, Tom has one major point: "You've got a disadvantage? Take advantage of it! People don't buy similarity. They buy differences." That is one great line.

Don't let cynicism eat your lunch. Don't allow the quicksand of self-pity to take you under. Someone is offering you a rope—take it! Grab on, hold on, and come back and help the rest of us get through our traumas. You have a distinctive message! If you could only get past your handicap, either physical or emotional, you would be amazed at how God could use you. Which brings me to the third and final question . . .

3. *Have you ever considered the impact your message would have on other hurting people?* You think it was easy writing this book? Hardly. All four of us wrote with agony and tears (literally). Each has cried and wept as we unearthed emotions we thought were buried. But we did it because we thought it might help someone else. If one person can find help and hope on our emotional dime, it has been worth the expenditure.

You have been set upon this earth as a one-of-a-kind jewel—forged through the refining fire of God's furnace—with the end result that when the SON-light of God's love hits your life, you will sparkle and gleam like you would never have believed.

Do you have a story? Isn't it about time you started using it for God's glory? How about starting right now . . .

96910.